180 Daily Guidance Lessons To

JUMP-START YOUR DAY!

180 Daily Lessons, 36 Weekly Topics,
Parent/Guardian Letters, and Classroom Activities
That Promote Respect, Individuality,
Compassion, Confidence, Strength, and Peace.

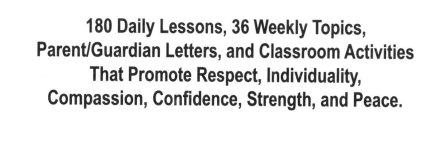

Tuesday
7

sday
8

Written by
Shannon Trice Black, M.Ed., LPC

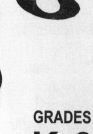

GRADES
K-6

180 DAILY GUIDANCE LESSONS TO JUMP-START YOUR DAY!

10-DIGIT ISBN: 1-57543-155-6   13-DIGIT ISBN: 978-1-57543-155-0

COPYRIGHT © 2007 MAR∗CO PRODUCTS, INC
Published by mar∗co products, inc.
1443 Old York Road
Warminster, PA 18974
1-800-448-2197
www.marcoproducts.com

Graphic Design: Cameon Funk

PRINTED IN THE U.S.A.

DEDICATION

This book is dedicated to the students and staff at
Byrd Elementary School in Goochland, Virginia,
who helped make these lessons fun for everyone!

ACKNOWLEDGMENTS

Thank you, Lord, for guiding me through my
decisions and carrying me through each day.

Thank you to my family—Margaret, Caroline, and Gary—
for your patience with me and for always showing me
the importance of family, laughter, and fun.

Thanks so much to Mama, Daddy, Grandma, and Jennifer.
Thanks for your support—even for all my crazy ideas!

Thanks so much to all my great girlfriends—
for your talks and support and for taking me out
every time I've needed a diversion.

CONTENTS

INTRODUCTION

Overview:

The *Jump-Start!* program is composed of 180 short daily lessons, weekly topics, parent letters, and follow-up classroom activities for elementary and middle school students. The daily lessons—which include student-inspiring role models, skits, and tips to be used at home and in school—may be read during morning announcements. They're a great way to start each day. The classroom activities may also be used during classroom guidance sessions. Weekly parent/guardian letters support the program and help reinforce the lessons. *Jump-Start!* is an easy-to-use, year-round program that will promote peace, empathy, individuality, strength, and friendship among students.

Rationale:

A proactive, preventive program, *Jump-Start!* focuses on the school as a whole and emphasizes behaviors that cultivate and support respect, friendship, individuality, and compassion. Daily lessons that include inspirational role models, fun and lively skits, and goals to achieve at home and in school teach and reinforce positive behaviors. In order to prevent such behaviors as aggression, bullying, violence, and relational aggression, we must teach our students to cultivate empathy and courage, to think about the feelings of others, respect themselves and others, and stand up for their own rights and the rights of others.

7

HOW TO USE THIS BOOK

Before You Begin:

This book is composed of 180 5-minute lessons and 36 weekly topics such as "Go Above and Beyond," "Have a Dream," and "Walk in Someone Else's Shoes." The program also contains weekly parent/guardian letters and follow-up activities that may be used by classroom teachers or in classroom guidance lessons. Schools may use such times as the morning announcements to provide these lessons, incentives, recognition, and rewards for all students.

Morning Announcements:

Morning announcements are an ideal time to present daily *Jump-Start!* lessons to the entire student body. This is a great way to start the day! At my school, I played crazy wake-up music to get everyone's attention before reading the short lesson. My students loved the music and looked forward to hearing each day's lesson.

Every Friday at my school, each classroom teacher nominates as *Student of the Week* whichever of his/her students best met the goal for that week. The following Monday, the names of student winners were announced. The winning students were called to the office, where they received award ribbons. Their pictures were taken and posted on our *Student Recognition Board.* This system worked well for our school, but ideas such as weekly awards luncheons, ice cream treats, or special privileges for recognized students may be more successful at your school.

Weekly Topics:

WEEK #	TOPIC
1	Include Everyone
2	Respectful Words
3	Reach Out
4	Make a Difference (Disciplined)
5	Help Others
6	Go Above and Beyond Perseverance/Disciplined ✓
7	Make a New Friend
8	Assert Yourself
9	Improve Our World
10	Act With Courage
11	Show Compassion
12	Be a Leader

180 Daily Guidance Lessons To Jump-Start Your Day! © 2007 Mar*co Products, Inc. 1.800.448.2197

13	Being Aware	
14	Walk in Someone Else's Shoes	TOLERANCE
15	Be Unique	
(16)	Do the Right Thing	R~
17	Be a Friend to Everyone	
(18)	Be Responsible	Responsibility
19	Seize the Day	
20	Listen to Others	
21	Have a Dream	
(22)	Be Honest	Integrity
23	Share Your Time	
24	Believe	
25	Try Something New	
26	Think Before Acting	
27	Do Something You Love	
28	Have an Open Mind	
29	Make Someone's Day	
30	Think Positive Thoughts	
(31)	Do Your Best	Excellence
32	Don't Give Up	Perseverance
33	Start Over	Perseverance
34	Forgive Others	
(35)	Achieve a Goal	Perseverance
36	Talk	

Weekly Schedule:

MON	TUES	WED	THURS	FRI
Recognition & Inspiration	Rationale	Role Models	At Home	What Would You Do?

Each week, each teacher will nominate one student from his/her classroom as *Student of the Week*. The nominated students will be recognized during Monday's morning announcements.

180 Daily Guidance Lessons To Jump-Start Your Day! © 2007 Mar*co Products, Inc. 1.800.448.2197

Weekly Format:

MONDAY
Recognition and Inspiration: Students nominated as *Student of the Week* for their performance of the previous week's goal are recognized. The weekly goal is announced, and its meaning is clarified for the students.

TUESDAY
Rationale: Why Should We Do This? explains the reason to strive for the goal.

WEDNESDAY
Role Models: Tidbits are related about famous people and others who do or have done a great job of achieving the weekly goal.

THURSDAY
At Home: Students are given an assignment concerning ways to achieve this goal at home and in school.

FRIDAY
What Would You Do? Students are selected to perform skits about ways to engage in positive behaviors. Each skit ends with the question *What would you do?* to help students think about the responsible choices they can make. *What Would You Do?* may also be used as a springboard for class discussions.

Letters to Parents/Guardians:

This book contains letters that provide parents/guardians with tips, ideas, and activities that help support and encourage the lesson of the week. At the beginning of each week, these letters may be copied and sent home with students.

Classroom Activities:

Each topic also includes classroom activities that may be conducted by classroom teachers or during classroom guidance lessons. These activities are wonderful tools to help teach and reinforce the topic of the week.

180 Daily Guidance Lessons To Jump-Start Your Day! © 2007 Mar∗co Products, Inc. 1.800.448.2197

JUMP-START!
WEEKLY LESSONS

INCLUDE EVERYONE

Monday: Recognition and Inspiration

This week, your goal as a student at _____ School is to *include everyone*. Make sure that you include everyone in your activities. If you see someone by him/herself at recess or lunch, make sure you ask that person to join you and your friends. It is each student's responsibility to include everyone in every activity. If you are playing basketball, for example, and someone is standing near the court and not playing, it is your responsibility to ask that student to play with you. Remember to *include everyone* today.

Tuesday: Why Should We Include Everyone?

By including everyone, we make sure that no one is left out of activities. If you've ever been the last one picked for a team, or if you've ever been told that you can't participate in a game, you know that being left out can make someone feel very lonely, sad, or angry. By including everyone, we are preventing bullying. We are preventing others from feeling isolated, lonely, and angry. This is your class, your school, and your responsibility. Remember to *include everyone* today.

Wednesday: Role Model

Our role model this week is Tiger Woods. Tiger Woods and his parents started The Tiger Woods Foundation, which helps disadvantaged children learn to play golf. Tiger Woods has included everyone by making sure that these kids can participate in activities they might otherwise not be able to enjoy. Please remember to be like Tiger Woods and *include everyone* today.

Thursday: At Home

You can work on including everyone at home by making sure that you let your brothers, sisters, cousins, and friends play with your toys and games—even when they annoy you! This can be especially difficult to do with family! Including everyone is not based on what we want or what we feel like doing. If we are very unselfish and think about the feelings of others, these decisions will make our world a better place. Remember to *include everyone* today.

180 Daily Guidance Lessons To Jump-Start Your Day! © 2007 Mar*co Products, Inc. 1.800.448.2197

Friday: What Would You Do?

William: Hey, Jahmal! Do you want to shoot some hoops?

Jahmal: Yeah, let's go!

William: Look, there's Craig, sitting by himself on the grass. Should we ask him to play?

Jahmal: I don't know. He's the worst at basketball! And sometimes he gets on my nerves.

William: I know, but we need to do the right thing.

What would you do?

Classroom Activities

Ball Toss Game: Play a short classroom game in which students throw a ball to one another and compliment the person who catches the toss. The ball may be thrown to each student only one time so that every student will be included.

Discussion and Writing/Drawing Activity: Have the students discuss, then draw or write about a time that they were not included in an activity. Then ask:

- How did you feel when you were not included?
- What would have made you feel better?
- How can you make sure that you always include everyone?
- Why do you think people sometimes exclude others?

13

LETTER TO PARENTS/GUARDIANS
WEEK 1: INCLUDE EVERYONE

Dear Parents/Guardians:

As part of JUMP-START! this week, our school is focusing on the importance of *including everyone.* Most of us have been left out of an activity at one time or another, and we know how lonely that can feel. We are trying to teach our students that it is their responsibility to include everyone. If our students see someone sitting alone at lunch, we want them to invite that person to sit with them. If our students see someone standing alone at recess, we want them to invite that student to play. Including everyone is not always easy. It takes courage and compassion. Our students must be willing to stop and think about the feelings of others.

Fun Family Tips:

◎ Encourage your children to include each other in their games and fun. Sibling rivalry and disputes are normal, but siblings should try to support one another.
◎ Talk to your child about a time when you were not included in an activity. Talk about the way you felt. Ask your child if he/she has ever felt this way and talk about ways to ensure that we include others.
◎ Praise your child for efforts he/she makes to include brothers, sisters, or classmates in activities.

Have a great week!

RESPECTFUL WORDS

Monday: Recognition and Inspiration

We would first like to congratulate last week's *Students of the Week,* who met our goal to *include everyone.* (Read students' names aloud.)

This week, your goal as a student at _____ School is to use *respectful words.* Make sure the words you use are words that help and encourage others. Use respectful words with friends, classmates, teachers, school staff, and families. Try to impress your teacher with your words today. Tell a friend you like her outfit. Tell another friend that you like his artwork.

Tuesday: Why Should We Use Respectful Words?

Respectful words encourage others and help them feel better about themselves. Disrespectful words can hurt and damage others, often causing people to react in anger or feel sadness. Most people have been damaged by someone else's words at some time. Things that people say when they are mad, or even just teasing, can hurt and damage others. People often say things before thinking about the impact their words can have on others. Make sure you use *respectful words* today!

Wednesday: Role Model

Oprah Winfrey is a wonderful role model for using respectful words. On *"Oprah,"* her talk show, she uses her words to encourage and help improve the lives of others. Her *Angel Network* reaches out and finds those in need, and Oprah donates much of her money to help others in need. Remember to be like Oprah and use *respectful words* today.

Thursday: At Home

At home tonight, tell something you like about someone in your family. Maybe your brother is great at playing games. Maybe your mom makes awesome macaroni and cheese. Sometimes we forget to tell our families about the things they do that make us happy. Don't forget to use *respectful words* today.

Friday: What Would You Do?

Trisha: Hey, Carla! Where did you learn to draw? Your artwork is terrible. I bet your mom won't hang that on the refrigerator!

Tara: I think Carla's drawings are pretty cool. They've got lots of color, and no one else has done anything like that.

Trisha: Oh, come on, Tara! You do *not* think Carla's pictures are good. Go ahead and tell her what they *really* look like. You know they look awful.

What would you do?

Classroom Activities

Respectful Words Hot Potato Game (EARLY ELEMENTARY): Pass a small ball around while music plays. When the music stops, the student who is holding the ball must say a respectful word.

Respectful Ball Toss Game (LATE ELEMENTARY, MIDDLE): Students throw a small ball to each other. The student who catches the ball must say a respectful word within 5 seconds. A student who drops the ball or who cannot think of a respectful word is out of the game.

JUMP-START!

LETTER TO PARENTS/GUARDIANS
WEEK 2: RESPECTFUL WORDS

Dear Parents/Guardians:

As part of JUMP-START! this week, our school is focusing on *respectful words.* Respectful words encourage people and help others feel good about themselves. Disrespectful words hurt and damage people. We want our students to make sure that they use words that help others.

Please encourage your child to think about the impact his/her words can have on others. Talk about how great it feels to receive compliments or praise.

Fun Family Tips:

◎ Have everyone in your family give each other family member one compliment before starting to eat dinner.
◎ Have a *Great Manners* contest. Reward your children for wonderful manners with small stickers or tokens. Have a family celebration when the children earn a certain number of stickers or tokens.

Thanks for your support!

REACH OUT

Monday: Recognition and Inspiration

We would first like to congratulate last week's *Students of the Week,* who met our goal to *use respectful words.*

This week, your goal as a student at _____ School is to *reach out* to others. Take a good look around and help others when they need something. Offer to help your teachers, bus drivers, custodians, cafeteria workers, and classmates. Remember to *reach out* to others today.

Tuesday: Why Should We Reach Out?

We often get so involved in our schoolwork and with our close friends that we don't notice everything else around us. Some people may be having a hard time, but we don't even see what's happening. It is important to care about everyone and to *reach out* to those in need. If you or someone else is being hurt or bullied, you need to seek adult help. If someone is feeling sad or lonely, you need to talk with that person and listen to how he/she is feeling. This is your school and these are your classmates. *Reach out* and help someone today.

Wednesday: Role Model

Corrie Ten Boom is a great example of someone who reached out to others. Corrie Ten Boom lived in Holland during the Holocaust and risked her life by hiding Jewish families in her home. Without her help, many of these people would have been captured and tortured, and some would have died. Corrie was taken to a concentration camp after it was discovered that she had been helping Jewish families. Even during her time in the concentration camp, Corrie reached out to others and helped them. *Reach out* to someone today!

Thursday: At Home

At home tonight, reach out to your family. Look around and see who might need a little help. Maybe your dad needs some help around the house. Maybe your brother or sister is having a hard time with homework. Remember to *reach out* to someone today!

180 Daily Guidance Lessons To Jump-Start Your Day! © 2007 Mar*co Products, Inc. 1.800.448.2197

Friday: What Would You Do?

Chris: Why is Tim standing over there by himself? Is something wrong?

BJ: I don't know. I guess he'll tell us if something's wrong.

Chris: I want to go over there and talk with him.

BJ: Come on! He'll tell you if he needs you. Let's go do something fun. I'm in a hurry! We don't have much time.

What would you do?

Classroom Activities

Classroom Chain: Give each child a slip of paper. Instruct each student to write down one way he/she can *reach out* to others. Make each slip of paper into a chain. Connect all the chains to create a long classroom chain.

Discussion: Discuss a time when someone *reached out* to you and helped you have a better day.

19

JUMP-START!

LETTER TO PARENTS/GUARDIANS
WEEK 3: REACH OUT

Dear Parents/Guardians:

As part of JUMP-START! this week, our school is focusing on *reaching out* to others. Reaching out to others helps us become aware of the needs of others and help others with these needs. It is easy to become so involved in our own worries and day-to-day activities that we don't notice things around us. Encourage your child to step back, look around, and reach out to others.

Fun Family Tips:

◎ At dinner, have each member of your family talk about one way he/she can reach out and help a family member. Have a celebration at the end of the week if everyone has done a great job of reaching out to others!
◎ Invite a neighbor or relative to join your family for dinner.
◎ Visit a nursing home. Spend some time just talking with the people who live there.

Have a great week!

MAKE A DIFFERENCE

Monday: Recognition and Inspiration

We would first like to congratulate last week's *Students of the Week,* who met our goal to *reach out* to others.

This week, your goal as a student at _____ School is to *make a difference.* We need to think about other people, our school, and our world. If something needs to be done, we need to do it. This is our world and we are responsible for it.

Tuesday: Why Should We Make a Difference?

Making a difference helps us change things in the lives of others. Maybe you don't like the way some students treat each other. The great thing is that YOU CAN make a difference by being an example to your friends of how everyone should be treated, even when others are not acting the same way. Making a difference takes faith and courage. Maybe you wish you could change something even bigger, like eliminating world hunger or poverty. You CAN make a difference! You can help people in need by volunteering your time, by donating your spare change, or by raising money. Be brave and *make a difference* today.

Wednesday: Role Model

Mia Hamm is an a outstanding professional soccer player who has used her fame and fortune to make a difference in our world. A member of the U.S. Women's National Soccer Team that won the Gold Medal in the 1996 Olympic Games, she started the Mia Hamm Foundation, which focuses on raising funds for and awareness of bone marrow transplant surgery and develops new opportunities for young women in sports. Be like Mia and *make a difference* today!

Thursday: At Home

You can make a difference at home by designating a jar or box for spare change you and your family members donate. Talk about what in the world you would like to see change. Research ways you can help make these changes happen. Donate your money to a cause that will *make a difference.* Start making a difference today!

Friday: What Would You Do?

Krissy: I am still so stuffed! We had a cookout last night, and you would not believe the food we had there. We had chicken, macaroni and cheese, watermelon, and corn. It was awesome!

Mequell: Stop! You're making me hungry, and we still have to sit in reading for an hour before lunch.

Krissy: I know. A whole hour to go before we get to eat again.

Mequell: You know, we only have to wait an hour. What about the people who lose everything they have because of a disaster like a hurricane? I wonder how many of them have been hungry.

Krissy: I know, that must be awful. But what can we do about it?

Mequell: I'm going to donate my snack money to the Red Cross every day for a month. The Red Cross helps people during times of crisis or disaster. I love to eat and I love snacks, but other people need that money more than I do.

What would you do?

Classroom Activity

Pick a Charity: Ask the students donate their spare change to a charity for a month. Have students research the charity. Talk about why this charity is important. Whom does it help? How does it help? Each week, tell the students how much money the class has raised. At the end of the month, have a celebration or party in honor of the charity the children have chosen.

180 Daily Guidance Lessons To Jump-Start Your Day! © 2007 Mar*co Products, Inc. 1.800.448.2197

JUMP-START!

LETTER TO PARENTS/GUARDIANS
WEEK 4: MAKE A DIFFERENCE

Dear Parents/Guardians:

As part of JUMP-START! this week, our school is focusing on *making a difference.* Making a difference helps us change things in the lives of others. If we don't like the way someone is being treated, we have the power to get help from an adult for that person. If we don't like the way something is happening in the world, we can help make a difference by volunteering our time or donating our spare change to charities. In order to make a difference, we need to be brave and believe that what we do is important. Encourage your child to make a difference at school, at home, and in the world around him/her.

Fun Family Tip:

◎ Make a difference in your community. Volunteer to take part in a community clean-up day or a charity event. You can spend the day working as a family and making a difference in the lives of others. Some families make it a holiday tradition to volunteer their time to help out in a soup kitchen or some other charitable effort. Why not give it a try?

Have a great week!

HELP OTHERS

Monday: Recognition and Inspiration

We would first like to congratulate last week's *Students of the Week,* who met our goal to *make a difference.*

This week, your goal as a student at _____School is to *help others.* When we help others, we are giving part of ourselves to someone else. We are willing to pause and think about the needs of others. We are willing to put the needs of someone else above our own. This week, you can try to help others in your class understand something, find something, or learn something new. Maybe you can help your brother or sister with homework or help an adult with a chore.

Tuesday: Why Should We Help Others?

Helping others lets people know they are not alone or powerless. Everyone needs help at one time or another. Think about a time when you did not understand the rules of a game, how to do a math problem, or how to read something. Think about a time when you needed help working something out with a friend or completing a chore or project. Think about how wonderful it is to have someone help you when you're frustrated. Make sure that you help others experience that same feeling. Helping others requires us to stop doing what we are doing (even if it is something fun) and concentrate on what someone else needs. Helping others requires us to be unselfish and caring. To be a good helper, we must provide assistance when people ask and offer help when we know someone is struggling—even if they don't ask for help. This week, make sure that you are ready and willing to help your friends, your classmates, your teachers, and your family. Ask the caring question, "What can I do to help you?"

Wednesday: Role Model

Our role model for this week is Tyra Banks, a famous fashion model who goes out of her way to help others. She created the TZONE Foundation to benefit disadvantaged teenage girls and fund programs and services that promote personal accountability, goal-setting, and healthy lifestyles. Tyra Banks hopes to help girls resist negative peer pressure, believe in themselves, and become confident leaders, and she established a camp that helps girls build trust, teamwork, and self-esteem. Tyra Banks sees girls who need help and responds to their needs. Make sure that you *help others* today.

180 Daily Guidance Lessons To Jump-Start Your Day! © 2007 Mar✶co Products, Inc. 1.800.448.2197

Thursday: At Home

At home tonight, you can practice the great gift of helping others by helping your family cook dinner or offering to help your brothers or sisters clean their rooms. Family members must be able to rely on each other for help. You must make sure that you are aware of and responding to the needs of your family members. Remember to always ask, "What can I do to help you?" Even when you don't feel like it! Remember to *help others* today!

Friday: What Would You Do?

Marcie: Let's go outside. Everyone is waiting for us to play *four-square.*

Tina: I can't. My mom said I have to clean my room before I go out to play.

Marcie: Come on! Everyone is waiting! If we don't go now, they'll start without us and we won't get to play. I've been waiting all day to do this!.

Tina: There's no way I can get this room straightened in a few minutes without some help.

What would you do?

Classroom Activities

Helpful Charades: On slips of paper, write descriptions of different scenarios that require help ("Kerri dropped her books in the hallway," for example). Put the slips in a bag, divide the class into groups, and have each group of students pick a scenario and act it out for the class—along with a way to help others in that situation. The other students can guess the different scenarios (like *charades*).

Writing Topic: Have the students write about a time when someone helped them learn something new, such as how to ride a bike, play an instrument, play a sport, or play a game.

180 Daily Guidance Lessons To Jump-Start Your Day! © 2007 Mar∗co Products, Inc. 1.800.448.2197

JUMP-START!

LETTER TO PARENTS/GUARDIANS
WEEK 5: HELP OTHERS

Dear Parents/Guardians:

As part of JUMP-START! this week, our school is focusing on *helping others.* Helping others lets people know that they are not alone or powerless. By helping others, we help prevent feelings of loneliness, frustration, and isolation. By helping others, we are acting unselfishly and giving our assistance and care to people.

Please encourage your child to help others at school and at home. Please encourage your child to be perceptive enough and brave enough to ask, "What can I do to help you?"

Fun Family Tips:

◎ For a change this week, let each of your children pick the chore he/she dislikes the most and get one of his/her siblings to help do it. Each child may pick only one chore. Reward your children for their positive attitudes and hard work.

◎ As a family, help someone in need by making a meal and delivering it to him/her. Or help someone in need with some chores around the house. Talk with your children about the importance of helping others. Praise your children when they help others.

Have a great week!

GO ABOVE AND BEYOND

Monday: Recognition and Inspiration

We would first like to congratulate last week's *Students of the Week,* who met our goal to *help others.*

This week, your goal as a student at _____ School is to *go above and beyond.* In order to go above and beyond, you must be willing to meet expectations and do even more than is required. Don't just "do" your classwork today. Do your best, make sure your handwriting is neat, and try to learn something new. When you are with your classmates, don't just be nice. *Go above and beyond* and try to help someone have a great day!

Tuesday: Why Should We Go Above and Beyond?

The challenge to go above and beyond requires that we do our best at all times. By going above and beyond, people act responsibly by doing their part and a little more! The more people who go above and beyond, the fewer problems our world will have. It is not enough to simply obey a rule or complete a task. We must go above and beyond. For example, if you know that someone has been bullying a person who rides your bus, it is not enough to make sure that *you* are obeying the bus rules. You must go above and beyond and let an adult know that someone is being bullied—even though you may be scared to do so. When you are with your friends, go above and beyond to get along. When you are doing your homework or classwork, go above and beyond to do a great job. Remember to *go above and beyond* today.

Wednesday: Role Model

Martin Luther King Jr. went above and beyond. Dr. King was a minister who did not "just" preach to his congregation. He went above and beyond and reached out to the world. He fought peacefully for the civil rights of African Americans. He also fought for peace for all nations. Act like Martin Luther King today and *go above and beyond* in your actions.

Thursday: At Home

At home tonight, practice going above and beyond. Don't clean your room by throwing things anywhere—organize it! Don't help your mom only when she asks you to do something—go

180 Daily Guidance Lessons To Jump-Start Your Day! © 2007 Mar⋆co Products, Inc. 1.800.448.2197

above and beyond and do your chores and well as something extra. Go above and beyond in trying to get along with your brothers and sisters—even when they're driving you crazy!

Friday: What Would You Do?

Trisha: I don't know what to do. My sister and I had a big fight this morning. She is so out of control! She just went off on me, and I did not do a thing to her.

Chris: Did you try to talk with her?

Trisha: Talk with her? No way! She is the one who messed up—not me. She owes me an apology.

Chris: Maybe you should try to talk with her—even if it wasn't your fault. You know, go above and beyond. You never know: It might even make you feel better.

What would you do?

Classroom Activities

Goal-Setting Charts: Have each student set a personal academic or social goal. Have the students create goal-setting charts that list the ways they can go above and beyond to reach these goals. After a week, collect the charts to see how the students are progressing toward their goals. Point out the successes that students have achieved. Encourage the students to continue going above and beyond.

Discussion or Writing Topic: Have the students discuss or write about:

- why it is difficult for people to go above and beyond.
- why some people have too much pride.
- why some people are afraid of failure.
- what holds people back from doing their best.

180 Daily Guidance Lessons To Jump-Start Your Day! © 2007 Mar*co Products, Inc. 1.800.448.2197

JUMP-START!

LETTER TO PARENTS/GUARDIANS
WEEK 6: GO ABOVE AND BEYOND

Dear Parents/Guardians:

As part of JUMP-START! this week, our school is focusing on *going above and beyond.* Going above and beyond requires that everyone do his/her part, plus a little more. Going above and beyond requires that people act responsibly and do their best. If everyone did his/her best, we would rarely encounter the attitude that "It's not my problem," and the world would be a much more peaceful place. Encourage your child to take a risk and go above and beyond in order to achieve a goal. We are often unsure of ourselves and afraid to take a risk to reach a goal. Talk with your child about things he/she would like to achieve.

Fun Family Tips:

◎ As a family, go above and beyond in helping someone out. Give someone a "great day." Maybe you have a neighbor with young children. You can give her a break by preparing a meal for her family or volunteering your family for a night of babysitting.

◎ Point out times when your child goes above and beyond. Praise him/her for these actions!

Thanks, and have a great week!

MAKE A NEW FRIEND

Monday: Recognition and Inspiration

We would first like to congratulate last week's *Students of the Week,* who met our goal to *go above and beyond.*

This week, your goal as a student at _____ School is to *make a new friend.* Making new friends is a great way to make our school a wonderful place for everyone. Even though you may know everyone in your class, you probably don't know everything about each of your classmates. By talking with people you normally don't hang out with, you can reach out and get to know someone new!

Tuesday: Why Should We Make a New Friend?

Making new friends prevents us from falling into the trap of "cliques" or groups where we isolate ourselves and don't talk with people who aren't part of our group. This behavior can often make others feel lonely and as if they don't belong. Making a new friend is an easy thing to do—but it is something we do not do very often. Try talking with someone in your class whom you do not usually spend time with. You may be amazed to find that you share similar interests. Eat lunch with someone different today or play with someone different at recess. Each person in your class is a unique individual who has great things to offer. *Make a new friend* today!

Wednesday: Role Model

Laila Najjar, a Palestinian Muslim, and Adi Frish, an Israeli Jew, are great role models for friendship. Because of hatred and violence, there is very little friendly contact between Palestinians and Israelis. However, Laila and Adi have developed a strong friendship. Both girls grew up in Oasis of Peace, a village where Israelis and Palestinians live together as neighbors and friends. Laila and Adi say that their friendship is based on mutual respect. Despite cultural pressure for the two to be enemies, these young women are able to see the importance of not judging others.

Thursday: At Home

At home tonight, you can practice making a new friend by calling a classmate you do not usually spend time with. You can invite someone you do not usually spend time with to come to your home. Or you can hang out with someone or a teammate you do not usually play with. Be brave and *make a new friend*. You will be pleasantly surprised to learn all the cool things your new friend has to offer!

Friday: What Would You Do?

TJ: Hey, Marcus, I can't wait to go outside for recess! It's an awesome day to play ball.

Marcus: Which kids should we pick for our team?

TJ: The usual gang, I guess. Ricky, Thomas, Adrian. You know, everyone we usually pick.

Marcus: What about that new kid, Terrance?

TJ: I don't know. He seems kind of weird.

Marcus: We really don't know much about him. He's probably just nervous. I think we should ask him.

What would you do?

Classroom Activities

Student Interviews: Pair each student with a partner. Have each pair of students interview each other, then have each student make a short presentation about his/her partner.

Discussion Questions: Discuss the following questions with the students:

- What do you think influences people when they choose their friends?
- How do you think groups of friends treat new students or students who don't normally hang out with them?
- What do you think can be done to improve friendships in our school?

180 Daily Guidance Lessons To Jump-Start Your Day! © 2007 Mar✶co Products, Inc. 1.800.448.2197

JUMP-START!

LETTER TO PARENTS/GUARDIANS
WEEK 7: MAKE A NEW FRIEND

Dear Parents/Guardians:

As part of JUMP-START! this week, our school is focusing on *making new friends.* Making new friends helps students get to know others and learn to include others in their activities. Emphasizing the importance of getting to know everyone prevents students from forming "cliques" or groups that do not include everyone. Please encourage your child to give everyone a chance!

Fun Family Tip:

◎ Here's a simple at-home activity that teaches your children the importance of getting to know the "inside" of someone, rather than judging others by how they look or the way they act:

Place your child's favorite snack or candy in a plain brown lunch bag. Place a rock or other heavy object in a gift bag. Let your child choose which bag he/she wants. (He/she will usually pick the gift bag.) After your child opens the gift bag and sees what it contains, give him/her the snack in the plain bag. Talk with your child about how we cannot judge what is inside something (like a bag) just by looking at it, just as we cannot judge a person's personality just by looking at him/her!

Thanks, and have a great week!

ASSERT YOURSELF

Monday: Recognition and Inspiration

We would first like to congratulate last week's *Students of the Week,* who met our goal to *make a new friend.*

This week, your goal as a student at _____ School is to *assert yourself.* Asserting yourself takes courage and confidence. Asserting yourself means that you believe in yourself and that you are willing to stand up for yourself and for others. *Assert yourself* today by answering a question in class, by playing a better game of ball, or by telling someone who is bothering you to stop what he/she is doing.

Tuesday: Why Should You Assert Yourself?

Asserting yourself lets people know that you have self-respect and that you will stand up for yourself. Asserting yourself is not the same as being aggressive or fighting. When we assert ourselves, we use statements such as, "Stop doing that" or "Leave me alone." Right now, in your classroom, practice making these two statements—and say them like you mean them! Don't say them in a shy, scared voice, but don't yell them as if you're looking for a fight. An assertive voice is a loud, clear voice that we use when looking right at someone—even when we are scared! Practice making these two statements once again. This time, practice with a partner! Have a great day—and don't forget to *assert yourself* today!

Wednesday: Role Model

Rosa Parks stood up for her rights and asserted herself in a non-violent manner. In December 1955, Rosa Parks boarded a bus in Alabama. During this time of segregation, African-Americans were supposed to sit in certain parts of buses and were supposed to give whites first choice of seating. When Rosa Parks refused to give up her seat to a white person, she was arrested and made history. This assertive, non-violent action led to a year-long boycott of buses by African-Americans in Alabama and spurred many people to learn more about the Civil Rights Movement or take part in it. Remember that your actions can be powerful, and you can have a great effect on others without being violent!

Thursday: At Home

You can assert yourself at home by standing up for yourself when your brothers or sisters make you angry. Instead of getting mad, simply look them in the face and say, "Stop it now." You don't even have to say it in a mean way—but say it like you mean it. Asserting yourself also means stating your opinions and thoughts. If your mom asks what you want for dinner,

180 Daily Guidance Lessons To Jump-Start Your Day! © 2007 Mar*co Products, Inc. 1.800.448.2197

don't just shrug your shoulders and say you don't know. *Assert yourself* by thinking about your answer and telling your mom what you would like.

Friday: What Would You Do?

Kenny: I am so sick of that guy on the bus! He really gets on my nerves. He never does anything terrible, like hitting me, but he always picks at me. I can't even talk with my friends because of him.

Lisa: What are you going to do? I think you should stand up for yourself.

Kenny: I want to! He's making me so mad! I feel like I'm going to lose my temper. But I don't want to be the one to get into trouble just because he's annoying.

Lisa: I don't mean that you should be violent or hurtful. But I think you should stand up for yourself by looking him right in the face and telling him to stop what he's doing. Say it like you mean it. You should say, "You need to STOP bothering me NOW!"

What would you do?

Classroom Activity

Journal Topic: Write about a time when you were afraid to stand up for yourself or a time when you did not do a good job of handling a conflict and ended up in trouble. Include what you wish you had said or done differently, how you think it would have changed the situation, why you think people have trouble standing up for themselves in non-violent ways, and what can be done to change this.

180 Daily Guidance Lessons To Jump-Start Your Day! © 2007 Mar✳co Products, Inc. 1.800.448.2197

JUMP-START!

LETTER TO PARENTS/GUARDIANS
WEEK 8: ASSERT YOURSELF

Dear Parents/Guardians:

As part of JUMP-START! this week, we are focusing on *asserting yourself.* Asserting yourself shows others that you respect yourself and will stand up for yourself. Asserting yourself is different from passive behaviors by people who may be too afraid and too quiet to stand up for their rights. Assertive behaviors are also very different from aggressive, violent behaviors that hurt others. Please talk with your child about the difference between these behaviors. Encourage your child to practice strong, assertive behaviors.

Fun Family Tip:

◎ Practice assertive behaviors with simple role-plays at the dinner table or even in the car. Have your child practice making assertive statements such as, "Stop that" or "Leave me alone." Reverse roles. Have your child be the "bully," and respond with appropriate assertive statements. Your child will get a big kick out of hearing your responses, and this will help him/her remember them better!

Have a great week!

IMPROVE OUR WORLD

Monday: Recognition and Inspiration

We would first like to congratulate last week's *Students of the Week,* who met our goal of *asserting themselves.*

This week, your goal as a student at _____ School is to help *improve our world.* Improving our world may seem like a huge task to even think about! However, it is the job of each child or adult to take care of our world's people, environment, relationships, and much, much more! It is up to you to think about things that YOU would like to see improved and changed. It is up to YOU to begin making those improvements, no matter how big or small they may be. Everyone can *improve our world.*

Tuesday: Why Should We Improve Our World?

Improving our world allows each person to take responsibility for things that he/she would like to see change. People often develop the "not my problem" attitude when they decide there is nothing they can do to change things they don't like. Imagine how great our world would be if everyone had the energy and the faith to step forward and do something about things he/she would like to improve. If you think that your lunchroom or school hallway needs a little bit of brightening up, for example, don't just complain about how it looks. This is your chance to do something about it. You could bring in your artwork, your pictures, or your ideas that can positively affect your school. This is just one example. Remember that you hold the keys and the ideas of ways to *improve our world.* Have the faith to do it today!

Wednesday: Role Model

Jourdan Urbach of Roslyn, New York dreamed of becoming a neurosurgeon so he could help sick children. He was only 7 years old, but he did not let his young age stop him from fulfilling his dream of helping children. Even though he was too young to become a doctor, he used the talents he had to help children in hospitals. Jourdan is an accomplished violinist who founded Children Helping Children, a musical charity that has raised more than one million dollars for pediatric divisions of hospitals and medical charities. Remember that you are never to young to *improve our world!*

180 Daily Guidance Lessons To Jump-Start Your Day! © 2007 Mar✳co Products, Inc. 1.800.448.2197

Thursday: At Home

At home tonight, you can talk with your family about ways that you can improve our world. Together, you can think of something that you would like to see happen and what you can do to help make it happen. It can be something as simple as planting flowers in your yard. Just think about how seeing beauty can brighten others' day as they walk or drive by!

Friday: What Would You Do?

Maurice: Where are you going?

Kendall: I'm going to the nursing home.

Maurice: Why are you going there? Is someone from your family there?

Kendall: No, I made some decorations and I'm taking them to the people who live there.

Maurice: Why did you do that?

Kendall: I just thought that they probably don't get to see their families very much and probably don't get very much company. They don't get to go out very often, either, so they have to look at the same things all the time. I figured I could visit and give them something to decorate their rooms a little. Do you want to help me?

What would you do?

Classroom Activities

School Beautification Project: As a class, have the students pick a beautification project for the school. They can work on this project, which might include essays on why the chosen area of the school needs to be changed and how the students would like to change it, pictures of how the area should look, and presentations of the entire process.

Class Discussion: Lead a class discussion on improving our world. Ask such questions as:

- What would you like to see change in our world?
- Why do you think this change would be a good thing?
- What could make this change happen?
- How can you help make this change happen?

180 Daily Guidance Lessons To Jump-Start Your Day! © 2007 Mar*co Products, Inc. 1.800.448.2197

JUMP-START!

LETTER TO PARENTS/GUARDIANS
WEEK 9: IMPROVE OUR WORLD

Dear Parents/Guardians:

As part of JUMP-START! this week, our school is focusing on *improving our world.* Improving our world helps people recognize and think about things other than ourselves. It helps us develop a proactive attitude rather than a passive "It's not my problem" attitude. We are never too young or too old to help improve our world. Improving our world is easy. No positive action is too small to help. Even picking up one piece of trash helps improve our world! Please continue to encourage your child to think about and do something about things in our world that need to be changed.

Fun Family Tips:

- Maybe your family can plant a garden. A garden is visually appealing, and you can donate part of the food you grow to people in need.
- When members of your family do things that help improve our world, notice and compliment them. Helping each other, cleaning up, being responsible—all of these things help improve our world!

Thanks, and have a great week!

ACT WITH COURAGE

Monday: Recognition and Inspiration

We would first like to congratulate last week's *Students of the Week,* who met our goal to *improve our world.*

This week, your goal as a student at _____ School is to *act with courage.* This sounds like a simple goal and many people say that they are brave and courageous. But acting with courage in difficult situations, such as times when we may be the only one standing up for something, is hard to do. Acting with courage takes practice and a belief that we are doing the right thing. It takes a lot of courage to do something when everyone else will laugh or tease us, but we know it is the right thing to do. It takes a great deal of courage not to go along with something that our friends are doing because we know it isn't right. Make sure that you *act with courage* today!

Tuesday: Why Should We Act With Courage?

Acting with courage helps us stand up for ourselves, stand up for others, and do the right thing—even if our friends are doing something different. People often think that brave people do not feel afraid or alone. This is not true! People who act with courage may feel scared or alone. The difference between someone who acts with courage and someone who does not is that the person who acts with courage takes a step forward, no matter how he/she is feeling, and acts with bravery. People who act with courage may care what others say or think about them, but they do not allow what others say or think to stop them from doing what they believe is right. Acting with courage is difficult, but it is a quality that you can develop. *Act with courage* today.

Wednesday: Role Model

As our role model of acting with courage, we will honor not one person, but many. Firefighters are an incredible example of acting with courage. They risk their lives every day to save others. Firefighters probably feel the same fear that everyone feels. But firefighters do not act on feelings of fear or run away at the sight of a fire. Imagine how horrible that would be! Instead, firefighters act with courage and do the right thing. No matter what they may be feeling, they help put out fires and save lives. Being a firefighter requires a great deal of courage. *Act with courage* today!

Thursday: At Home

At home tonight, you can act with courage by trying something new. Maybe you've always wanted to learn how to sing, paint, draw, or play a sport. Try something that you have been scared to try and see how it goes. You may be surprised at the results! Even if you are nervous or scared, *act with courage* and try it!

Friday: What Would You Do?

Chris: Hey, guys! Are you ready to eat lunch?

Graham: Look at Tim's pants! He wears those awful things every day. He's disgusting! Why is he sitting near us? Hey, Tim! Go away!

Chase: He's so gross, I can't stand to even sit near him. Chris, go tell Tim to get away from us.

Chris: I'm not going to say that.

Graham: Why? Are you Tim's friend? Are you gross and disgusting, too? Maybe we can't sit with you, either, if you can't tell him to leave.

What would you do?

Classroom Activities

Hero Project: Have the students research and talk about heroes. Each student may pick one hero and use the Internet or the library to look up facts about that person. Have the students write short, descriptive essays about their heroes and draw pictures of them. Students may then tell the class about their heroes.

Class Discussion: Lead a class discussion. Ask:

- What do you think makes a person a hero?
- Who are some people who are heroes to you?
- Talk about a time when you were scared to do something and did it anyway.
- Talk about some things you would like to do, but have been afraid to try.

180 Daily Guidance Lessons To Jump-Start Your Day! © 2007 Mar*co Products, Inc. 1.800.448.2197

LETTER TO PARENTS/GUARDIANS
WEEK 10: ACT WITH COURAGE

Dear Parents/Guardians:

As part of JUMP-START! this week, our school is focusing on *acting with courage.* Acting with courage helps people do brave things, despite what others may say, do, or think about them. If we do the right thing, even though friends tease or laugh at us, most episodes of "ganging up" on someone will be eliminated. Acting with courage is very difficult to do. Everyone feels scared about doing something that goes against what friends are doing. Please encourage your child to act with courage, even when he/she is worried about what others are thinking or saying.

Fun Family Tips:

◎ As a family, watch a movie about a hero. Talk about how the person acting with courage might have felt. Remind your child that the hero probably felt fear, but still acted with courage. Talk about how it is OK to be scared.

◎ Talk about things that you, as an adult, have been afraid to try or do. Talk about times when you have acted with courage to try these things, despite your fears.

Thanks, and have a great week!

WEEK 11
SHOW COMPASSION

Monday: Recognition and Inspiration

We would first like to congratulate last week's *Students of the Week*, who met our goal to *act with courage*.

This week, your goal as a student at _____ School is to *show compassion*. We show compassion by reaching out to others and letting others know that we care for them. To feel and show compassion, we must be able to think about how others feel. We can show compassion to other students by helping them with their work. We can show compassion by reaching out when someone is upset. We can show compassion even when someone is not showing that he/she is sad, even though something unfair or hurtful has happened. For example, if someone says hurtful things to another student, we can say something to that student like, "Are you OK?" or "I'm sorry about what that person said to you." It really helps to know that others care about us and we are not alone.

Tuesday: Why Should We Show Compassion?

Showing compassion lets people know they are not alone. Unless others show compassion, we may feel isolated and believe that we don't have any friends. When we show compassion, we can eliminate feelings of isolation and loneliness. Make sure that you show compassion by reaching out to others who have been hurt or left out. *Show compassion* to others with kind words and actions today!

Wednesday: Role Model

Our role model for this week is Mackenzie Snyder of Bowie, Maryland. At the age of 7, Mackenzie learned that many children in foster care have to pack their belongings in garbage bags when they move to new foster homes. Mackenzie was filled with compassion for these children, and wanted to do something to help them. She collected and sent duffel bags and backpacks and stuffed animals to foster children. Inside each bag, she placed a personal note. Mackenzie's compassionate project is now known as Children to Children and has provided bags for more than 28,000 foster children all over the United States. Act like Mackenzie and *show compassion* today!

180 Daily Guidance Lessons To Jump-Start Your Day! © 2007 Mar✶co Products, Inc. 1.800.448.2197

Thursday: At Home

At home, you can show compassion to your brothers, sisters, parents, grandparents, and other family members. Try helping your brothers or sisters with something that is hard for them. Show compassion to your tired mom or dad by offering to clean part of the house or do laundry. Visit your grandparents and talk with them. They might be lonely and would probably love to spend time with you. *Show compassion* everywhere you go!

Friday: What Would You Do?

Joaquin: Get away from us, Rachel! You are so gross, no one wants to hang out with you.

Latisha: Hey, Rachel, I'm sorry about what Joaquin said to you. Don't listen to him.

Rachel: I feel sometimes like what they say is true. No one wants to be around me. It seems like no one hangs out with me at recess.

Latisha: Well, I will. Come on, I'll walk with you out there.

Rachel: Thanks.

What would you do?

Classroom Activities

Class Discussion: Lead a class discussion. Ask:

- Why do you think people do not show compassion to others?
- How can we help people at our school show compassion?
- What do you think would improve if people were more compassionate?

Compassion Basket: Have each student write down such compassionate statements as, "Hang in there!" or "I'm sorry about that." and drop them into a basket. Each day, pick one of the compassionate statements and talk about how students could use this statement to help someone.

180 Daily Guidance Lessons To Jump-Start Your Day! © 2007 Mar*co Products, Inc. 1.800.448.2197

JUMP-START!

LETTER TO PARENTS/GUARDIANS
WEEK 11: SHOW COMPASSION

Dear Parents/Guardians:

As part of JUMP-START! this week, our school is focusing on *showing compassion* to others. Showing compassion lets others know that they are not alone and that someone cares about them. Showing compassion eliminates the loneliness and isolation felt by people who are bullied or picked on by others. Showing compassion helps people reach out to others and promotes empathy. Please encourage your child to show compassion in his/her actions toward others. Often people act quickly before thinking about their actions. It's important to help children think about how their actions affect others and how they can help, not hurt, others.

Fun Family Tip:

◎ Practice making compassionate statements with your family. You can even practice this in the car as a game. Each person can make a compassionate statement. See how many turns your family can take before running out of compassionate statements. After finishing one game, begin again. Practicing making compassionate statements will help your child learn to use them easily with friends and family.

Thanks, and have a great week!

BE A LEADER

Monday: Recognition and Inspiration

We would first like to congratulate last week's *Students of the Week,* who met our goal to *show compassion.*

This week, your goal as a student at _____ School is to *be a leader.* Learning to be a leader requires us to act on our own, without always having the approval of our friends. Many times, we want to be followers rather than leaders. When we are followers, we don't need to make many decisions. We just go along with the crowd. The problem with being followers is that we may end up doing things that are not right for us. To be leaders, we must believe in ourselves. Even if something feels difficult or scary, leaders forge ahead with the belief that they are doing the right thing. Be a leader today at recess by playing a game that you want to play, even if it is not what everyone else seems to want to do. You might be surprised to find that others will join you. Be a leader today at lunch by talking with people you do not always talk with. Don't be afraid to change or to do things a little differently. *Be a leader* today.

Tuesday: Why Should We Be Leaders?

People who act as leaders are not as likely to go along with the crowd. People who are leaders are not afraid to make their own decisions based on their own desires, rather than on what they think everyone else will be doing. People who are leaders will not join in when someone is bothering another person. People who are leaders will talk with someone even if other people laugh at them. People who are leaders pick their friends based on mutual interests and character, not on how popular the other person is. Be brave and *be a leader* today!

Wednesday: Role Model

Our role model for this week is Susan B. Anthony, who helped women obtain the same rights as men. When Susan B. Anthony was born in 1820, women did not have the right to vote. Susan B. Anthony had to deal with ridicule and even being arrested in her fight for women's rights. Nonetheless, she continued to be a leader. Remember to *be a leader* today!

Thursday: At Home

At home, you can be a leader by taking the initiative to do something. Maybe you would like to plant a garden. Instead of just thinking about it, figure out what you need, ask permission from your mom and dad, and prepare to work on your garden. Your whole family might want to join in the fun. If you are bored or restless, don't complain to your parents. *Be a leader* and figure out something productive to do. You and your family might be amazed to find out how great your ideas can be! Show off your leadership skills tonight!

Friday: What Would You Do?

Hashim: I think we should figure out a way to get out of going to class today. I just can't deal with one more day of listening to that teacher talk.

Tara: I know! I am sick of it, too. Maybe we should hide in the bathroom and then sneak out.

Hashim: Yeah, let's do it. Come on, Heather, let's go.

Heather: I don't know. I'm not so sure that's the best idea. I think we should go to class and just get our work done as quickly as possible. Our teacher promised us yesterday that we could have extra recess if we did all our work today. If we skip class, we'll probably get caught, and we definitely won't get to go outside. I think we should just go in there and deal with it so we can all go outside. I'm dying for a game of soccer.

What would you do?

Classroom Activity

Writing Topic/Class Discussion: Have the students write about or describe a person they think is a great leader, the characteristics that make this person a great leader, and how this person has helped others.

JUMP-START!

LETTER TO PARENTS/GUARDIANS
WEEK 12: BE A LEADER

Dear Parents/Guardians:

As part of JUMP-START! this week, our school is focusing on *being a leader.* Being a leader helps people follow their own consciences and their own ideas, rather than going along with others. Leaders will not pick on or harass someone just because others are doing so. Leaders are more likely to stand up for themselves and others, and to reach out to those in need. Being a leader is difficult at times, because it requires that we act differently from others. That can be very hard for children, especially with peer pressure. Praise your child when you notice leadership skills. Encourage your child to be a leader and to be proud!

Fun Family Tip:

◎ Each day of the week, designate one person of your family to be the *Leader of the Day.* Allow this person to pick one activity for your family to do together. It can be a 5-minute game or an outing. By giving your child practice in being a leader, you will help him/her develop confidence and leadership skills.

Thanks, and have a great week!

BEING AWARE

Monday: Recognition and Inspiration

We would first like to congratulate last week's *Students of the Week,* who met our goal of *being a leader.*

This week, your goal as a student at _____ School is *being aware.* Being aware means noticing the things that are going on around us and not ignoring them. In order to be aware, we must pay attention to how others are feeling and what is happening in their lives. It is easy to just think about ourselves and the things *we* are feeling and needing. Being aware requires us to forget about our own needs for a while. You may be surprised to find that when you focus on others, your problems don't seem so important. And sometimes they have a way of working themselves out! Focus on *being aware* today!

Tuesday: Why Should We Be Aware?

Being aware helps people notice if others are being left out, picked on, or not treated fairly. Being aware helps us think about others' feelings and their circumstances. If we do not focus on ourselves, but on being aware of others' needs, we can be a friend to someone, stand up for someone, talk with someone who is feeling down, or help someone out. Make a point of *being aware* of what's going on today!

Wednesday: Role Model

Our role model for this week is Mattie Stepanek, who began composing inspirational poetry when he was only 3 years old. Mattie Stepanek suffered from dysautonomic mitochondrial myopathy, which confined him to a wheelchair. Nonetheless, Mattie was aware of others and of the world around him. By the time he passed away in June 2004, Mattie had written seven books of inspirational writings of peace and love for one another. Instead of concentrating on his own difficulties and suffering, Mattie made it a point of to be aware of needs outside himself and was able to contribute greatly to our world.

Thursday: At Home

At home tonight, you can show your family your ability to be aware by noticing a few things in your house that need to be done. Your parents will be pleasantly surprised if you pick up and

180 Daily Guidance Lessons To Jump-Start Your Day! © 2007 Mar✶co Products, Inc. 1.800.448.2197

throw away trash you didn't leave on the floor. Your mom may cry tears of joy if you notice dirty dishes in the sink and wash them. Your brother may decide not to bother you for a while if you put his laundry away. Practice *being aware* tonight!

Friday: What Would You Do?

Hailey: I have so much math homework to do, I can't believe it. And my mom left a huge list of chores I have to get done or I can't go anywhere fun tomorrow. I hate doing all this stuff! What are you doing?

Felicia: I'm volunteering to tutor some kids in reading.

Hailey: Why are you doing that? I don't even have enough time to do my own stuff. And the little bit of time I have left, I need to be able to watch my shows. You'll never get everything done! What's wrong with you?

Felicia: I always had trouble with reading, and I heard some kids talking on the bus about how much they don't like reading. So I asked their teacher if I could help out.

What would you do?

Classroom Activities

Poetry Writing: Talk about how the role model of the week, Mattie Stepanek, began writing inspirational poems about peace and love at the age of 3. You may want to share some of Mattie's poems with the class. Mattie's books are published by Andrews McMeel Publications and are: *Heartsongs*; *Loving Through Heartsongs*; *Celebrate Through Heartsongs*; *Hope Through Heartsongs*; *Reflections Of A Peacemaker: A Portrait Through Heartsongs*; and *Just Peace: A Message Of Hope*, written with President Jimmy Carter. Ask the students to each write a poem that requires being aware of things other than themselves. Have your students share their poems with the class.

Class Discussion: When the students have completed their poems, ask:

- How did these poems help you become more aware?
- Which poem affected you the most? Explain how it affected you.
- Are you inspired by any of these poems to do anything differently? If so, please explain.

180 Daily Guidance Lessons To Jump-Start Your Day! © 2007 Mar✲co Products, Inc. 1.800.448.2197

JUMP-START!

LETTER TO PARENTS/GUARDIANS
WEEK 13: BEING AWARE

Dear Parents/Guardians:

As part of JUMP-START this week, our school is focusing on *being aware.* Being aware helps people focus on things other than themselves. By focusing on others and the world around us, we are able to notice people who are lonely, people who are picked on, people who need help, people who need to talk, and more. It is easy to get so wrapped up in our own struggles and dilemmas, that we don't see those around us. Encourage your child to be aware of others' needs and the needs of the world. Talk with your child about things you notice. Children base many of their behaviors on those of their parents!

Fun Family Tip:

◎ Play a quick game of awareness with your family. Blindfold each member of your family, one at a time, and give him/her objects to feel. The purpose of the game is to guess what the object is without being able to see it. Talk about how difficult it is to notice things without looking at them and how much easier it is to just open our eyes and look. Explain how this game is similar to what we can do in our daily lives—simply opening our eyes and looking around us!

Thanks, and have a great week!

WALK IN SOMEONE ELSE'S SHOES

Monday: Recognition and Inspiration

We would first like to congratulate last week's *Students of the Week,* who met our goal of *being aware.*

This week, your goal as a student at _____ School is to *walk in someone else's shoes.* You won't *really* walk in someone else's shoes. But you will imagine what life would be like if you were someone else. It is hard for us to imagine our lives as anything other than what they are—our families, our friends, our school, our community, and our country. But in order to become more caring, empathetic people, it is important for us to be able to imagine what life would be like for someone else. Take a *walk in someone else's shoes* today.

Tuesday: Why Should We Walk in Someone Else's Shoes?

Imagining a walk in the shoes of someone else helps us make sure that our actions will only help, not hurt, others. It also helps us understand others. When you see the way someone is acting, don't immediately judge and react. Take a step back and think about what this person's life is like. Does he/she have a lot of friends? Does he/she have help at home? Does he/she seem happy? These things make a big difference. Taking a walk in someone else's shoes will help you see another person's needs and be able to help him/her. Imagine your walk today!

Wednesday: Role Model

Nelson Mandela is an inspirational role model for walking in someone else's shoes because he was willing to spend many years of his life in prison in order to fight for freedom and equality in South Africa. During his time in prison, Nelson Mandela was not willing to compromise his values or his fight against violence in order to obtain his freedom. Instead, Nelson Mandela was a great source of strength, education, and inspiration for the other prisoners. Imagine a *walk in someone else's shoes* today!

Thursday: At Home

At home tonight, switch jobs with one of your brothers or sisters or one of your parents. If your mom usually cooks dinner and you clean up, ask her to switch with you. Or if your brother usually takes out the trash and you feed the animals, ask him to trade. We often think that another person has a much easier job or a much easier time in life. Tonight, find out for yourself what someone else's job is really like and talk about it!

180 Daily Guidance Lessons To Jump-Start Your Day! © 2007 Mar★co Products, Inc. 1.800.448.2197

Friday: What Would You Do?

Orlando: That new kid is so weird! He's always staring at everyone. His clothes are really strange, too.

Polly: Give him a break! He just moved here.

Orlando: I know, but does he have to be such a weirdo? I don't want anyone hanging around with me who looks or acts like that. He talks funny, too.

Polly: Have you ever thought about the reason he talks like that? It isn't weird. It's his accent from the country where he was born and lived until he moved here. And can you imagine coming to this school from a different country? I'm sure our clothes are somewhat different than what he wore at home. He's probably staring because he's trying to fit in and understand what's going on.

What would you do?

Classroom Activity

International Costume Day: Assign each class in your school a different country. Help the students research different customs and styles of dress for that country. Help your students assemble costumes for their country, wear them to school, and present information about the customs of their country. Students may prepare food from different countries and visit each other's classes for an imaginary walk in another land!

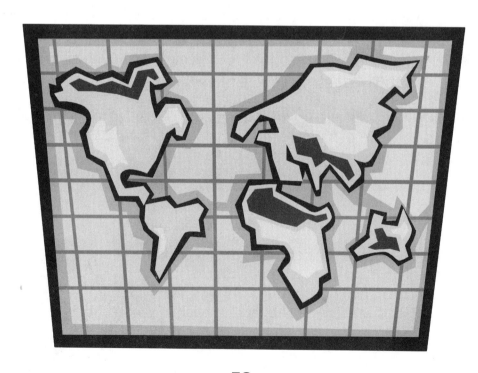

180 Daily Guidance Lessons To Jump-Start Your Day! © 2007 Mar*co Products, Inc. 1.800.448.2197

JUMP-START!

LETTER TO PARENTS/GUARDIANS
WEEK 14: WALK IN SOMEONE ELSE'S SHOES

Dear Parents/Guardians:

As part of JUMP-START! this week, we are focusing on *walking in someone else's shoes.* Imagining a walk in someone else's shoes helps us not judge others. It also helps us become more empathetic and caring toward others. Talk with your child about what life is like for children in different countries. Talk with your child about what life is like for children in different parts of America. Make sure your child is aware that everyone faces different challenges. Encourage your child to be open to others' differences and to care about the needs of others.

Fun Family Tip:

◎ As a family, prepare a meal that is associated with another country. For example, you could prepare Thai, Chinese, Mexican, or Indian food. While enjoying the meal, spend some time talking about the culture and customs of the country. Talk about what you imagine life might be like in this country.

Thanks, and have a great week!

BE UNIQUE

Monday: Recognition and Inspiration

We would first like to congratulate last week's *Students of the Week, who* met our goal to *walk in someone else's shoes.*

This week, your goal as a student at _____ School is to *be unique.* We often try to do things the "popular" way and focus on what everyone else seems to be doing. We can become afraid to do things differently and too scared to try something new. Too often, we compare ourselves to others and expect that everyone should be alike. When this happens, we lose our individuality, the quality that makes each of us special. Our challenge this week is to *be unique.* Embrace the personal characteristics that make you different from others. Show off your unique characteristics to the world!

Tuesday: Why Should We Be Unique?

Being unique helps us show off our differences and do the things we want to do, rather than the things that are viewed as popular. When we embrace our individuality, our self-esteem increases. So does our respect for differences in others. When we behave in a unique way, rather than going along with what everyone else is doing, we can prevent situations such as someone bullying another person just because others are doing it. Think about how you can *be unique* and all you have to offer today!

Wednesday: Role Model

Our role model for this week is Deborah Sampson. Born in 1760, Deborah felt led to support her country during the Revolutionary War. She posed as a man, enlisted in the army, and fought for freedom from British rule. After being wounded in battle, Deborah used a penknife and a needle to remove a bullet from her leg so the doctor would not discover her secret. Her wound did not heal properly, and she was hospitalized with a fever. She was discovered to be a woman and was honorably discharged from the army. Deborah Sampson is remembered as the first American woman to disguise herself as a man and fight as a soldier. Don't be afraid to *be unique* today!

180 Daily Guidance Lessons To Jump-Start Your Day! © 2007 Mar*co Products, Inc. 1.800.448.2197

Thursday: At Home

At home, you can be unique by concentrating on the things you love to do. Brothers and sisters often compare themselves to one another and even compete with each other. Think about what YOU enjoy doing and do it well, rather than comparing yourself to anyone else in your family. Families would be very boring if everyone did everything the same way. For example, maybe your sister is great in soccer and you like soccer, but it's not your favorite thing. Don't get down on yourself. Instead, think about what you really enjoy. Maybe it's art or reading or talking and listening with friends. Be proud of what you love and be proud of your uniqueness.

Friday: What Would You Do?

Tina: Are you planning on playing softball this spring?

Sierra: I don't know. I didn't really like it last year.

Tina: Come one, Sierra! Everyone is doing it. What else will you do? All our friends are going to be out there! It will be so much fun.

Sierra: I was thinking about taking piano lessons. I've always wanted to learn to play the piano.

Tina: Why would you do that? Piano lessons aren't fun at all! You can't hang out with anyone. Don't you want to have any friends or any fun?

What would you do?

Classroom Activity

I Am Unique Activity: Have each student create a life-size cutout displaying his/her uniqueness. Give each student a large piece of butcher paper. Have the students lie on the paper and trace each other's outlines. After cutting out their outlines, students may decorate their forms with descriptions and pictures of their unique characteristics. For example, a person who enjoys music might draw musical notes somewhere on the cutout. After completing the project, students may present their cutouts to the class.

180 Daily Guidance Lessons To Jump-Start Your Day! © 2007 Mar*co Products, Inc. 1.800.448.2197

JUMP-START!
LETTER TO PARENTS/GUARDIANS
WEEK 15: BE UNIQUE

Dear Parents/Guardians:

As part of JUMP-START! this week, we are focusing on *being unique.* Being unique helps us feel good about our differences and respect the differences in others. People who aren't afraid to be unique are less inclined to go along with the crowd and are not afraid to do the right thing. It is very difficult to be unique in today's society, because people often strive to belong to one social group or another.

Fun Family Tip:

◎ Have each member of your family describe his/her unique characteristics. Then have each other member of your family say what he/she thinks makes that individual unique. It will be wonderful to hear what each person has to say about him/herself and what each person has to say about each other family member. We too rarely take the time to say these things to one another. Take a few minutes to embrace your family's uniqueness today!

Thanks, and have a great week!

DO THE RIGHT THING

Monday: Recognition and Inspiration

We would first like to congratulate last week's *Students of the Week,* who met our goal to *be unique.*

This week, your goal as a student at _____ School is to *do the right thing.* In this program, we have often talked about how doing the right thing is a daily challenge and should be a daily goal for everyone. It may sometimes seem easier to do something that isn't right. Maybe doing the right thing will take a lot of time and work or maybe our friends will laugh at us if we do the right thing. However, if we don't do the right thing, guilt, loss of trust, disappointment, hurt feelings, anger, fights, punishments, and many more problems may arise. Stop and ask yourself today if you are *doing the right thing!*

Tuesday: Why Should We Do the Right Thing?

Doing the right thing prevents such actions as hurtful teasing, harassing, spreading rumors, isolating others, and bullying. By doing the right thing, we can make sure that we are helping, not hurting, others. We can also ensure that we are being a great example to others. Many times, if one person is willing to step forward and do the right thing, others will follow. *Do the right thing* today!

Wednesday: Role Model

Our role model for this week is Abraham Lincoln, who was the 16th president of the United States. During the Civil War, Abraham Lincoln did the right thing by issuing the *Emancipation Proclamation,* which freed slaves. Think about what a difference that made in our country! Make sure you *do the right thing* today!

Thursday: At Home

You can make sure you do the right thing at home by talking with your parents when you are faced with difficult decisions. It is sometimes hard to figure out how to do the right thing, but an adult can often help us make the right decision. Talk with your parents tonight about tough decisions you have to make about your friends, your schoolwork, or anything!

Friday: What Would You Do?

Jamison: Are you going to the football game on Saturday? Everyone is going to be there!

Lilly: I can't figure out what to do. I really want to go to the football game, but I think I'm supposed to baby-sit.

Jamison: Don't baby-sit. That's so boring! Why don't you just say that you're sick or that your parents won't let you baby-sit? Then we can go to the game together. It will be great!

What would you do?

Classroom Activities

Decision-Making Tic-Tac-Toe: Divide the class into two groups and identify one group as "X" and the other as "O." Draw a tic-tac-toe grid on the chalkboard. Play a game of tic-tac-toe. Decide which group will go first. Select one student from that group and describe a simple scenario in which he/she must decide how to do the right thing. If the answer is correct, the student may choose where to put the "X" or "O." If the answer is not correct, the student may not place a letter on the grid. Move on to the next group and continue the game, alternating between the two groups until one achieves tic-tac-toe.

Discussion: After completing one or more rounds of the game, ask:

- How do you decide how to do the right thing in different situations?
- Can you describe a time when it was difficult for you to do the right thing?

180 Daily Guidance Lessons To Jump-Start Your Day! © 2007 Mar∗co Products, Inc. 1.800.448.2197

JUMP-START!

LETTER TO PARENTS/GUARDIANS
WEEK 16: DO THE RIGHT THING

Dear Parents/Guardians:

As part of JUMP-START! this week, we are focusing on *doing the right thing.* Doing the right thing helps us think about whether we're making the right decisions. Making the right decision often takes more time, is harder to do, and requires more thought. But making the right decision saves many people from being hurt and is the better thing to do. Talk with your child about the importance of thinking about choices and doing the right thing. Notice and praise your child when he/she does the right thing.

Talk with your child about times when you have had difficulty making the right decision. Talk about a time when you made the right choice and a time when you made the wrong choice. Explain that we all make mistakes at times and sometimes make bad choices. But tell your child that we learn from our mistakes and learn to make better choices. Encourage your child to talk with you about difficult decisions that he/she faces.

Thanks, and have a great week!

BE A FRIEND TO EVERYONE

Monday: Recognition and Inspiration

We would first like to congratulate last week's *Students of the Week,* who met our goal to *do the right thing.*

This week, your goal as a student at _____ School is to *be a friend to everyone.* Being a friend to everyone sounds like a very simple task. But to REALLY be everyone's friend requires that we be unselfish, caring, good listeners, aware of the needs of others, and brave. We often limit ourselves to groups of friends, which keeps us from getting to know many other people. By being a friend to everyone, we open ourselves up to new people and new experiences. We have to be willing to share our friends with others and not get jealous. We must be willing to spend some time with someone we don't know as well as our closest friends, which may feel uncomfortable at first. We have to be open and accepting of everyone, not just certain groups of people. *Be a friend to everyone,* and you will add much to your life and to the lives of others!

Tuesday: Why Should We Be a Friend to Everyone?

Being a friend to everyone is a good way to prevent loneliness, isolation, discrimination, and prejudice. Being a friend to everyone prevents us from judging people before getting to know them. Furthermore, by being a friend to everyone, we don't form groups that exclude others. When we work on becoming everyone's friend, prejudice and discrimination will begin to disappear, leaving more friendships and peace in their place. *Be a friend to everyone* today!

Wednesday: Role Model

Our role model for this week is Kristi Yamaguchi, a champion figure skater who won an Olympic Gold medal in 1992. In 1996, Kristi founded the Always Dream Foundation to support organizations that have a positive influence on children. The Foundation's goal is to continue to provide funds for a variety of programs designed to inspire and embrace the hopes and dreams of children and teens. Through it, Kristi Yamaguchi demonstrates being a friend to everyone by reaching out to others, not discriminating, and including everyone. Make sure that you are a friend to everyone as well!

Thursday: At Home

At home you can be a friend to everyone in all the extracurricular activities that you enjoy. If you play sports, are part of a club, or belong to a youth group, you can be a friend to everyone. Don't hang out just with the kids who go to your school or who are your neighbors. Make sure that you are open to getting to know everyone. Make sure that you are willing to *be a friend to everyone* around you. Give everyone a chance today!

Friday: What Would You Do?

Katie: Why are you talking with those girls on the other cheerleading squad? Those girls don't go to our school.

Cindy: I was just getting to know them a little better. I was hoping we could all hang out.

Katie: Why do you need to hang out with them? You already have friends from our school.

Cindy: I like getting to know other people. And I think it's a good idea to talk with everyone.

Katie: Well, I don't see why you need to talk with them. I have all the friends I need.

What would you do?

Classroom Activity

Pen Pal Class Project: Have your students practice being friends with everyone by participating in a pen pal project. Pair each student with a student from another class in your school, another school in your area, or even from another country. Each month, help your students write letters to their pen pals. Teach your students to ask questions that will help them learn more about their pen pals. Help your students write appropriate information about themselves.

61

JUMP-START!

LETTER TO PARENTS/GUARDIANS
WEEK 17: BE A FRIEND TO EVERYONE

Dear Parents/Guardians:

As part of JUMP-START! this week, we are focusing on *being a friend to everyone*. Being a friend to everyone helps us reach out to include others. Being a friend to everyone helps us all get along and prevents loneliness. In order to be a friend to everyone, we must be willing to share our friends and our time with each other. We need to be unselfish and be willing to reach out to others.

Please encourage your child to be brave enough and caring enough to be a friend to everyone. Talk with your child about the importance of having friends. Help your child practice friendship skills. Praise your child when you see him/her reaching out to, talking with, or making friends with others!

Fun Family Tip:

◎ Ask your child to name every student in his/her homeroom or who takes part in one of his/her extracurricular activities. Have your child name something he/she likes about each student. Challenge your child to learn one new thing about each student this week. Reward your child if he/she learns one new thing about each student! Explain to your child that learning about others is a good way to be a friend to everyone!

Thanks, and have a great week!

BE RESPONSIBLE

Monday: Recognition and Inspiration

We would first like to congratulate last week's *Students of the Week,* who met our goal to *be a friend to everyone.*

This week, your goal as a student at _____ School is to *be responsible.* Being responsible means doing the things we are supposed to do, when we are supposed to do them. People who are responsible are trustworthy and obey rules, even when they don't feel like doing so. Responsible people do the right thing simply because it's the right thing to do. Amaze your teachers and your friends today by being responsible. Turn your work in on time—before your teacher asks for it. If you tell your friend you are going to play football during recess, do it! If you tell your friend you will sit beside her on the bus, don't change your mind and sit beside someone else. Don't forget to *be responsible* today!

Tuesday: Why Should We Be Responsible?

Being responsible helps prevent disappointment and hurt feelings, because responsible people do the things they promise to do and the things that are expected of them. Responsible people take ownership of their actions and don't blame others for their choices, which helps make others more careful and thoughtful about what they do. Irresponsible people often act without thinking about the effect their actions can have on others, which can cause problems. Make sure that your actions are responsible today.

Wednesday: Role Model

Our role model for this week is Pat Tillman. Pat was on his way to a promising football career with the Arizona Cardinals. In 2002, he chose to leave the NFL and enlist in the Army to help fight for our country. Pat gave up a great deal of money and fame when he left football. Pat is our role model for the week because he did what he thought was the responsible thing to do. Unfortunately, Pat Tillman was killed in Afghanistan in 2004. We honor Pat and all others who serve and have served our country.

Thursday: At Home

At home you can be responsible by doing what is expected of you, before your parents have to remind you to do it. Imagine how excited your parents will be if they see you attacking your homework before they have started nagging you. Think about how peaceful your night will be if your parents are not fussing at you to clean your room, because you have already straightened it. Think about how happy your parents will be if you do what they ask without arguing or questioning. See what happens in your house if you decide to be responsible!

Friday: What Would You Do?

Antonio: What are you doing after school? Do you want to come over to my house?

Sunita: I'm supposed to vacuum the living room this afternoon.

Antonio: Come over right after school, you can vacuum later.

Sunita: I don't know. I was thinking of vacuuming right after school, because the house is really a mess and I know it's driving my mom crazy. She's been working a lot lately.

Antonio: Well, did she say you HAVE to do it BEFORE you can go anywhere? Or just sometime today?

Sunita: I guess just sometime. But I feel like it would be best to do it first. I'd have so much more fun at your house if I knew it was finished. And I'd know it would be one thing my mom wouldn't have to worry about.

Anthony: Well, if I didn't HAVE to do it right away, I'd just go play.

What would you do?

Classroom Activity

Class Discussion: Talk about the importance of school rules. Ask:

- What rules at school do you think are most important? Explain why you think these rules are important.
- What rules at school do you think are hard to obey? Why do you think these rules are difficult to follow?
- Do you think it is important to obey school rules that you don't agree with? Why or why not?

Talk about what would happen at school if people obeyed only the rules they liked.

180 Daily Guidance Lessons To Jump-Start Your Day! © 2007 Mar✳co Products, Inc. 1.800.448.2197

JUMP-START!

LETTER TO PARENTS/GUARDIANS
WEEK 18: BE RESPONSIBLE

Dear Parents/Guardians:

As part of JUMP-START! this week, our school is focusing on *being responsible.* Being responsible prevents bullying, because it helps us do the things we are supposed to do and helps us take ownership of our own actions. When we do, we are more likely to think about what we're supposed to do and the effect our actions can have on others. We often act without thinking about how our actions can hurt other people. Talk with your child about the importance of being responsible. Explain that being responsible means doing the right thing, even when we don't feel like it. Praise your child when he/she acts responsibly.

Fun Family Tip:

◎ During a meal or in the car, talk about what responsibility means to each member of your family. Talk about the things many adults have to do for their families. For example, many adults in families have jobs. Responsible adults go to work every day and arrive on time. Talk about what it would be like if you woke up one day and just stayed in bed because you felt tired or if you went to work and did not do something your boss asked because you did not want to do it. Talk about what it would be like if everyone in your family acted irresponsibly for one whole day. Imagine all the disasters that could take place!

Thanks, and have a great week!

SEIZE THE DAY

Monday: Recognition and Inspiration

We would first like to congratulate last week's *Students of the Week,* who met our goal of *being responsible*.

This week, your goal as a student at _____ School is to *seize the day.* Seizing the day means being willing to take charge, do something differently, make a change, or make the most of a positive situation. Seizing the day requires energy, awareness, confidence, and faith. In order to seize the day, you must be willing to take some risks and do things that might be difficult. For example, maybe you are struggling in reading. Seize the day and get some extra help from your teacher, a tutor, your parents, or another student. Maybe you are struggling with making or keeping friends. Seize the day and talk with people or get help with friendship skills from an adult. Don't just let the problem go on. Do something about it. Think about something you need to do or want to do and *seize the day* by doing it today!

Tuesday: Why Should We Seize the Day?

Seizing the day helps us do something, rather than passively sitting back. For example, by seizing the day, someone who is being picked on can stand up for him/herself or seek help from an adult. Someone who has not been doing a good job of being a friend to everyone can seize the day and be a friend to everyone today. Someone who is lonely can seize the day by using good friendship skills to talk with others. People who seize the day do not postpone dealing with a problem or assume that they are just stuck with it. Instead, they show initiative and deal with it! *Seize the day* today!

Wednesday: Role Model

Our role models for this week are Kevin Stephan and Penny Brown of Buffalo, New York. When Kevin was 11 years old, he was hit in the chest with a baseball bat and his heart stopped. Penny Brown, a nurse whose son played on the same team as Kevin's younger brother, performed CPR on Kevin, and saved his life. Seven years later, Kevin was working in a restaurant where a woman began choking on her food. Kevin, a volunteer firefighter, rushed out of the kitchen to perform the Heimlich maneuver. His quick actions saved the woman's life. It turned out that the woman was Penny Brown, who had saved Kevin's life seven years earlier! These two role models, who saved each other's lives, are wonderful examples of people who seized the day. If either of them had wasted a moment, a life might have been lost.

Thursday: At Home

At home, you can seize the day by thinking about something you have always wanted to try or wanted to do differently. Maybe it is a hobby, sport, or craft. Seize the day today and try it. Don't put it off one more day. We often postpone trying something new because we are afraid we will fail, so we never get the opportunity to experience many fun, exciting things. You may be amazed to find your hidden talents and abilities. Seize the day today!

Friday: What Would You Do?

Chelsea: Have you ever noticed that nobody sits next to Melody? She just sits by herself during lunch and recess, and she always looks so sad.

Peyton: Melody is just weird. That's why nobody sits with her.

Chelsea: I've been thinking about her and what it would feel like to be her and have no one to sit with. I was thinking about asking her to sit with us today.

Peyton: No way! Lunch is so much fun! Don't ruin it. Besides, we ALWAYS sit with Meredith and Gabby and talk. I don't want someone else messing everything up.

Chelsea: I know, but we sit together every day. I just really think we should change things a little. I think we need to think about what the right thing to do would be.

What would you do?

Classroom Activity

Writing Topic: Have each student write a descriptive paper explaining:

- What *seize the day* means to him/her.
- What are some ways he/she has seized the day in the past.
- What are some ways he/she would like to seize the day.
- Why he/she thinks it is important that people seize the day.

180 Daily Guidance Lessons To Jump-Start Your Day! © 2007 Mar*co Products, Inc. 1.800.448.2197

**LETTER TO PARENTS/GUARDIANS
WEEK 19: SEIZE THE DAY**

Dear Parents/Guardians:

As part of JUMP-START! this week, we are focusing on *seizing the day.* Seizing the day helps us build confidence in ourselves and to make active choices, instead of sitting back and reacting passively. Someone who is being picked on, instead of accepting that treatment, can seize the day and plan an assertive way to deal with the problem—whether it be standing up for him/herself, seeking adult help, or making new friends. People who seize the day pursue activities that interest them, which helps build self-esteem. Encourage your child not to postpone positive decisions and actions. Ask your child about anything that he/she wants to do but is nervous, scared, or unsure about doing. Help your child develop a plan for seizing the day.

Fun Family Tip:

◎ Through discussion, the Internet, or even a movie, learn about someone who seized the day by making decisions that could have changed his/her life, as well as the lives of others. Many famous or not-so-famous heroes are people who made courageous decisions that saved the lives of others.

Have a great week!

LISTEN TO OTHERS

Monday: Recognition and Inspiration

We would first like to congratulate last week's *Students of the Week,* who met our goal of *seizing the day.*

This week, your goal as a student at _____ Elementary School is to *listen to others.* By listening to others, we can become better classmates, better friends, better students, better brothers and sisters, better children to our parents, and better citizens of our world. It is very easy to ignore what others are saying because we are concentrating on our own needs. It takes discipline and compassion to really listen to what others are saying. Really listen to your teacher's instructions today. Your teacher will be amazed at how quickly you remember and follow all the directions. Really listen to what your friend is saying today. It will help your friendship when your friend sees how much you care about his/her problem. *Listen to others* today!

Tuesday: Why Should We Listen To Others?

Listening to others helps us pay attention to their needs, rather than focusing on ourselves. When we pay attention to what someone else is saying and doing, we are acting in a caring manner. The more we care about others, the less we will hurt one another. People who hurt or lash out at others are often in pain and may need some compassion and care. If someone begins showing them some attention and listening to them, the hurtful behaviors may be eliminated. People who take the time to listen to others help prevent loneliness, isolation, bullying, aggression, and violence. Make sure that you *listen to others* today!

Wednesday: Role Model

Our role model for this week is Connie Chung, who is an excellent example of someone who listens to others. Connie Chung was the first Asian Pacific anchorwoman on national television. People often think that successful reporters and journalists are the ones who ask the right questions. However, listening to the answers is just as important as asking the right questions. People who are being interviewed need to feel comfortable enough to talk and reveal information. Someone who is really listening can show the other person that he/she is interested in the response. *Listen to others* today!

Thursday: At Home

At home, you can listen to others by paying attention to what your parents say. Kids sometimes "tune out" some of the things their parents are saying and parents have to repeat a request or question many times. When parents have to repeat themselves, they often get frustrated or angry, which frustrates and angers the kids. By really listening the first time, you can save yourself, as well as your parents, a lot of unhappiness. Your house will be a much more peaceful place and people will enjoy being around each other much more. Listen to your parents today!

Friday: What Would You Do?

Isabella: Why do you think Joslyn has her head on her desk?

Selma: I don't know. I think she said something about her sister being mean to her. I wasn't really paying attention. I was thinking about the party on Saturday. Are you going to it? I think a lot of people are going to be there.

Isabella: Right now, I'm not thinking about the party. I want to go over and talk with Joslyn. She looks really upset. She probably needs to talk.

Selma: We don't have time for that. I don't want to listen to her problems right now. They're her problems, not mine.

Isabella: Well, I think she probably needs someone to talk with and to listen to the things that are bothering her.

What would you do?

Classroom Activity

Class Discussion: Ask the students:

- Do you think it is more important to be a good talker or a good listener? Explain why.
- How can you tell if someone is really listening to you? What does his/her face look like?
- How can you tell if someone is not listening to you?
- Have you ever been hurt when someone you were trying to talk with did not listen to you? What happened?
- Why do you think it is sometimes hard to listen?
- How can you be a better listener?

180 Daily Guidance Lessons To Jump-Start Your Day! © 2007 Mar*co Products, Inc. 1.800.448.2197

JUMP-START!

**LETTER TO PARENTS/GUARDIANS
WEEK 20: BE A GOOD LISTENER**

Dear Parents/Guardians:

As part of JUMP-START! this week, we are focusing on *being a good listener*. Good listeners show compassion and care when they really pay attention to someone talking about his/her problems. Good listeners help prevent loneliness and isolation, because they let others know that they are not alone in their struggles. Talk with your child about the importance of being a good listener to others. Talk about things like eye contact and not interrupting.

Fun Family Tip:

◎ With your child, pick an elderly relative or friend to call. Help your child think of appropriate questions to ask the other person in a conversation. Encourage your child to be a good listener. Afterward, talk about the importance of being a good listener and how being a good listener can help prevent loneliness.

Thanks, and have a great week!

HAVE A DREAM

Monday: Recognition and Inspiration

We would first like to congratulate last week's *Students of the Week,* who met our goal of *being good listeners.*

This week, your goal as a student at _____ School is to *have a dream.* Dreams are things we wish we could do, but may not know how to do. Think about some things you think sound pretty cool. It may be your dream to be an actor or actress. You may dream of being a painter or a baseball player, and you may not have any idea how to make these dreams come true. Don't give up on your dreams! Everyone has to start somewhere. If you're interested in something, begin exploring it and figuring out a way to make small pieces of your dream come true. Start today!

Tuesday: Why Should We Have a Dream?

Having a dream helps build confidence and self-esteem. Having dreams keeps people focused and excited. Dreams motivate us to do our best and to achieve our goals. Don't put limits on your dreams. Dream big and go after your dream. You can accomplish many things if you just try. Don't be scared to try something new. Think about your dreams and what you want to achieve today!

Wednesday: Role Model

Our role model for this week is Anne Sullivan. In 1887, she met Helen Keller who was blind, deaf, and could not speak or understand language. Despite Helen's handicaps, Anne believed that Helen could learn to communicate and to read. Anne's dreams came true and Helen learned to understand words, read Braille, and communicate through sign language. Even though many people had struggled without success to help Helen, Anne refused to give up on her dream. Be like Anne and *have a dream* today.

Thursday: At Home

At home, you can help inspire everyone in your family to go after his/her dreams. Even adults have dreams! Talk with your parents about the dreams they had as children. Ask your parents about the dreams they still have. Share some of your dreams with your brothers and sisters. Encourage each other. Respect each other's dreams, even if they sound silly or unbelievable. Try to help one other come up with plans to achieve these dreams. The impossible sometimes becomes possible with the help of others. Share your dreams tonight!

180 Daily Guidance Lessons To Jump-Start Your Day! © 2007 Mar∗co Products, Inc. 1.800.448.2197

Friday: What Would You Do?

Taryn: What are you doing?

Bettina: I'm practicing my golf swing.

Taryn: Why are you doing that? You don't know how to play golf.

Bettina: I know I don't know how to play golf! That's why I'm practicing. I'm trying to learn.

Taryn: Why do you want to play golf? Your parents are never going to pay for you to actually take lessons or really go golfing.

Bettina: I'm just interested in it—I think it's a really cool sport.

Taryn: Well, I think you are just wasting your time.

What would you do?

Classroom Activity

Dream Collage: Have each student make a personal dream collage. Students may cut pictures from magazines or draw pictures to create a collage filled with images of things they dream about doing. Let each student share his/her dream collage with the class.

180 Daily Guidance Lessons To Jump-Start Your Day! © 2007 Mar*co Products, Inc. 1.800.448.2197

JUMP-START!

LETTER TO PARENTS/GUARDIANS
WEEK 21: HAVE A DREAM

Dear Parents/Guardians:

As part of JUMP-START! this week, we are focusing on *having a dream*. Having a dream helps us focus on achieving a goal. Having dreams builds confidence and gives us something to be excited about. Encourage your child to have dreams, even if his/her dreams do not seem realistic. It is important for everyone, even adults, to have dreams. Dreams give us hope and keep us motivated. Try not to change your child's dreams, but help him/her learn more about the things in which he/she is interested.

Fun Family Tip:

◎ Visit your local library with your child. Help your child research and learn more about his/her dreams and goals. For example, if your child is interested in dance, find and check out books about dance. Use the Internet for additional resources. Your respect and support for your child's dreams will help build your child's confidence and self-esteem.

Thanks, and have a great week!

BE HONEST

Monday: Recognition and Inspiration

We would first like to congratulate last week's *Students of the Week,* who met our goal of *having a dream.*

This week, your goal as a student at _____ School is to *be honest.* Being honest sounds like a simple thing to do. However, if we really think about it, most of us will realize that we struggle with complete honesty. We may tell small lies to keep us or others out of trouble. We might not correct a sales clerk who doesn't charge us enough money. We might borrow things we don't plan to return. We need to think about being honest and make a decision to tell the truth. We need to tell the truth, despite the consequences, simply because telling the truth is right thing to do. Make sure to *be honest* today!

Tuesday: Why Should We Be Honest?

Being honest helps prevent hurtful, untrue rumors. Being honest helps people tell each other the truth and only say truthful things about each other. Verbal bullying—saying things to and about others that are meant to harm—can be very hurtful. Honesty helps build trust and loyalty between people and helps us believe in and count on one another. Even though it may be difficult to not join in when others are saying untruthful things about someone, make sure that you are honest and trustworthy.

Wednesday: Role Model

Our role model for this week is Benjamin Franklin, who was an inventor, a scientist, a writer, and a statesman. Benjamin Franklin included many moral lessons and teachings in his writings. He encouraged people to be honest, upstanding citizens. In one of his famous quotes, Benjamin Franklin wrote, "Honesty is the best policy." Follow Benjamin Franklin's advice today and make honesty *your* best policy.

Thursday: At Home

At home, you can help your entire family with your honesty. If you are honest with your parents, they will trust you and give you more freedom to make decisions. Being honest will show your parents that they can depend on you. Even though you may be tempted to lie sometimes to avoid trouble, make sure that you tell the truth. If you are dishonest, your parents will not be able to believe your words and will not have confidence in your actions. Be honest with your brothers and sisters and let them know that they can count on you. Honesty will help improve your relationship with everyone in your family. Think before you speak or act, and make sure you are *being honest!*

Friday: What Would You Do?

Corina: I am dreading going home today. My teacher wrote my parents a letter about the assignments I didn't turn in.

Niko: Why didn't you turn them in?

Corina: I just cannot stand doing all that work! I've been talking on the phone a lot lately, and I just haven't finished my work. My parents don't know that I didn't do it.

Niko: Why don't you just tell your parents that you did the work, but you lost it? They won't be nearly as upset at you if you lost your work instead of just not doing it.

What would you do?

Classroom Activities

Vocabulary Builder: Have the students define and use each of the following words in a sentence: *truth, dependable, trust, lie, cheat, fact, fiction, reliable,* and *responsible.* Practice these words with your class daily.

Class Discussion: Discuss how each of the vocabulary words relates to *honesty.*

76

JUMP-START!

LETTER TO PARENTS/GUARDIANS
WEEK 22: BE HONEST

Dear Parents/Guardians:

As part of JUMP-START! this week, we are focusing on *being honest.* Honesty helps eliminate hurtful lies and rumors that contribute to cliques, isolation, bullying, and aggression. Encourage your child to be honest in everything he/she does or says. Telling a lie is often a quick, seemingly easy choice when faced with a difficult situation. Explain to your child that dishonesty causes more problems by decreasing trust and often makes it necessary to tell more lies to help hide the truth. Praise your child for his/her honest actions.

Fun Family Tip:

◎ At dinner or in the car, discuss *honesty* with your family. Talk about such situations as finding something and deciding whether to keep it. Is it honest to take a CD that you find at school? Is it honest to say you are going to do something that you know you will not do (such as a chore or a sport)? Suggest different scenarios to your family and encourage everyone to discuss why these situations are or are not honest.

Thanks, and have a great week!

SHARE YOUR TIME

Monday: Recognition and Inspiration

We would first like to congratulate last week's *Students of the Week,* who met our goal of *being honest.*

This week, your goal as a student at _____ School is to *share your time.* Our lives are so busy with our own needs, that it is sometimes hard to share our time with others. Time is one of the most important gifts we can give someone else. A few minutes of our time can help someone complete a task or cheer up someone who needs a friend. Take a few moments today to talk with someone in your class who is looking a little down. Take the time to speak with your teachers. Share your time with your classmates, your teachers, and your family today.

Tuesday: Why Should We Share Our Time?

Sharing time helps us act in an unselfish way and reach out to others. Sharing time promotes friendship and prevents loneliness and isolation. Sharing time doesn't cost money, and you don't have to be an adult to do it. Anyone can share time! We just have to be willing. When a classmate needs help with something or just needs to talk, give him/her your time. We often think that we're too busy and can help later, but later may be too late. *Share your time* today!.

Wednesday: Role Model

Our role model for this week is Shaquille O'Neal, the famous basketball player. Not only does Shaquille O'Neal support charities, such as by making a one million dollar donation to the Boys and Girls Clubs of America, he donates his time. Donating time is something we can all do, and time can often help people more than any amount of money. Be like Shaquille and *share your time* today!

Thursday: At Home

At home you can share your time with your parents or grandparents. When adults ask us about our day, we often give them very short answers and very little information. Share your time with an adult tonight and tell him/her about your school day. Talk about your favorite class. Talk about what subject is difficult for you. Talk about your friends. Talk about what you'd like to do tomorrow. Ask questions about the adult's day. It may amaze you to see how much someone appreciates you sharing your time, simply talking!

180 Daily Guidance Lessons To Jump-Start Your Day! © 2007 Mar⋆co Products, Inc. 1.800.448.2197

Friday: What Would You Do?

Jeremiah: What are you doing after school? Do you want to come over and hang out?

Henry: I'm supposed to be going to visit my grandmother.

Jeremiah: Can't you come to my house instead? Why do you have to go over there?

Henry: I don't *have* to go over to her house. I go over there once a week to visit because she's lonely and she likes to see me. It's important to her, and I like making her happy.

Jeremiah: I think you should come to my house. You can go to your grandmother's house some other day.

What would you do?

Classroom Activity

Class Trip: Take a class trip to a nursing home. Before you go, help your students practice appropriate ways to act and talk with the residents. Students can prepare cards or practice a special song to perform. Stress the importance of sharing time with people. Explain that many people in nursing homes are separated from their families and friends and are often lonely. Our time is one of the greatest gifts we can give someone.

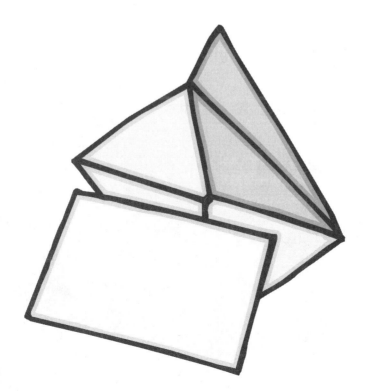

180 Daily Guidance Lessons To Jump-Start Your Day! © 2007 Mar∗co Products, Inc. 1.800.448.2197

JUMP-START!

LETTER TO PARENTS/GUARDIANS
WEEK 23: SHARE YOUR TIME

Dear Parents/Guardians:

As part of JUMP-START! this week, we are focusing on *sharing our time.* Sharing our time helps us think about the needs of others, rather than ourselves. Sharing our time helps us reach out and help others. In our fast-paced world, we often get so busy that we don't spend enough time with our loved ones. We race around from place to place and project to project. We forget about the importance of simply stopping and spending time with someone. Spend some time with your child and talk about how time is one of the most valuable gifts we can give someone.

Fun Family Tip:

◎ Before each of your children goes to bed, spend a few minutes reading, talking, or cuddling with him/her. Children often talk about important things at night. Use this time as a positive time, not a time for discipline. It is great for kids to go to bed on a loving, positive note, even if they have had a rough day. These few minutes can make a big difference in your relationship with your child.

Thanks, and have a great week!

BELIEVE

Monday: Recognition and Inspiration

We would first like to congratulate last week's *Students of the Week,* who met our goal of *sharing your time.*

This week, your goal as a student at _____ School is to *believe.* Believing in ourselves, in others, in a dream, and in a goal is important for all of us. We often get frustrated and have difficulty believing and trusting in ourselves and in others. Believing in something gives us goals to dream about and people to count on. Believe in your friends and encourage them. Believe in yourself and know that you can succeed. Start *believing* today!

Tuesday: Why Should We Believe?

Believing in ourselves and others helps gives us hope and helps us not become discouraged. Believing in ourselves increases self-esteem and self-confidence. Believing in dreams and goals helps us feel good about ourselves and helps us to focus on the things that are important to us. Believing requires faith and courage. It is often difficult to continue to believe, and it can be easy to give up. Don't stop believing. Keep going, and you may be amazed at the great things that happen to you and to others!

Wednesday: Role Model

Our role model for this week is Jackie Joyner-Kersee, a track star who competed in four different Olympic Games. Jackie believed in herself and believed she could succeed. She won six Olympic medals. She also founded the Jackie Joyner Kersee Youth Center Foundation, which helps prepare boys and girls to become productive adults. Her foundation helps kids believe in themselves and believe that they can succeed. Believe in yourself and help others to believe in themselves!

Thursday: At Home

At home you can practice believing in others by supporting your brothers and sisters in something they are trying to do. Believe in them and encourage them to do their best. It helps so much to have someone cheering you on! Your brothers and sisters will greatly appreciate your support. People who believe in themselves and who have others believing in them often achieve more than they ever thought they would. Show your family how you can *believe* today!

Friday: What Would You Do?

Hans: Where are you going?

Sammy: I'm going to the pool for swim team practice.

Hans: Why are you going to swim team practice? You don't usually swim very much.

Sammy: I know I haven't always been a great swimmer, but I've been working on my swimming and I really believe I can do better. I *want* to do better. I know I'll be slow, but this is something I've always wanted to do. So I'm believing and doing it. I could really use your support! Do you want to go to the pool with me?

What would you do?

Classroom Activity

Class Project: Have the students research famous people of the present and past who have used their beliefs to help change our world. Create a class collage with pictures and short paragraphs about each of the famous believers. Discuss the importance of each of these people believing in him/herself.

180 Daily Guidance Lessons To Jump-Start Your Day! © 2007 Mar∗co Products, Inc. 1.800.448.2197

JUMP-START!

LETTER TO PARENTS/GUARDIANS
WEEK 24: BELIEVE

Dear Parents/Guardians:

As part of JUMP-START! this week, we are focusing on *believing.* Believing in oneself and others helps prevent low self-esteem and gives us hope. It is important for us to believe in ourselves, in others, and in our goals and dreams. Encourage your child to have the faith and courage to believe. We often get discouraged and frustrated, and this makes believing difficult. Be a great example to your child by showing your belief in him/her. Knowing that someone believes in him/her can greatly boost a child's confidence level.

Fun Family Tip:

◎ As a family, spend some time talking about things that each family member believes in for him/herself as well as for each other. Talk about times when it has been difficult to believe. Talk about the importance of not giving up and of continuing to believe. Encourage each other and believe in each other. Make sure your family members know that you believe in each other.

Thanks, and have a great week!

WEEK 25
TRY SOMETHING NEW

Monday: Recognition and Inspiration

We would first like to congratulate last week's *Students of the Week,* who met our goal of *believing*.

This week, your goal as a student at _____ School is to *try something new*. We often get so used to doing the same things in the same way that we don't try new things. It can be difficult to break out of a safe routine, but new experiences have a lot to offer. Without trying new things, how could you find a new favorite food or a new fun friend or a hidden talent? Be brave and *try something new* today. Hang out with someone you don't always talk with, play a different game, try a new sport, eat something different. And have some fun!

Tuesday: Why Should We Try Something New?

Trying something new prevents people from sticking with the same groups of friends, who can form cliques that can lead to bullying. Trying something new gives people the courage to have lots of different friends and to not be afraid to break away from a group that may have a negative influence. Try something new today by sitting beside someone you don't normally sit with on the bus or hanging out with someone different during recess. Different people can offer new, exciting experiences. Be brave and *try something new* today!

Wednesday: Role Model

Our role model for this week is George Washington Carver. George Washington Carver was born in Missouri in 1864. As a child, he was greatly interested in plants and learned to read and write at home. The first college he attended did not offer science courses, so he studied piano and the arts. He transferred to Iowa Agricultural College, where he earned a Bachelor of Science degree. George Washington Carver tried something new when he developed a system of crop rotation that changed the way farmers in the southern states grew peanuts, sweet potatoes, peas, pecans, and other crops. He also discovered how to derive 325 products from peanuts and hundreds more from other crops. He was the first African-American to become a professor at Iowa College. Be like George Washington Carver and *try something new* today!

Thursday: At Home

At home you can surprise your parents by trying something new. Imagine your mom's face if you cleaned up your room BEFORE you went outside to play. Just think about how great it would be to listen to her praising you for doing a great job instead of nagging you to clean your room. Or you can get your parents to help you try a new sport or hobby. Talk with your parents about things you'd like to do and figure out a way to try to do them!

Friday: What Would You Do?

Gregory: What's that thing in your hand?

Marcus: It's a box of pastels.

Gregory: What are pastels?

Marcus: They're like crayons, only way cooler. I'm trying to make a picture for my mom for her birthday.

Gregory: Do you know how to do that?

Marcus: No, but I'm trying to learn.

Gregory: I don't know if you should try out something new for your mom's birthday. Why don't you just make her a regular card? What if this drawing looks weird?

What would you do?

Classroom Activity

New Experiences: Take a picture of each student in your class trying to do something new. For example, maybe one student wants to try tennis. Take a picture of him/her holding a tennis racket. Have each student write a descriptive paper about what he/she is trying to do and why he/she is trying to do it. Have the students explain whether they liked the new experience and what could have made the experience better for them. The students should also write about the differences between what they expected the new experience to be like and what the experience actually was like for them.

JUMP-START!

**LETTER TO PARENTS/GUARDIANS
WEEK 25: TRY SOMETHING NEW**

Dear Parents/Guardians:

As part of JUMP-START! this week, we are focusing on *trying something new.* Trying something helps us become brave and confident. New experiences help us become open-minded, which helps prevent discrimination. People who are open to trying new things are also open to making new friends, which promotes friendship. Encourage your child to be brave enough to try new things—new foods, new games, new books, new hobbies, new friends, and more. We sometimes do not want to try new things simply because we're scared that we won't like the new experience. But if we don't try new things, we won't discover many new things we might love. You and your child can experience something new!

Fun Family Tip:

◎ Think of something new you would like to try as a family. Maybe it is a new food. Maybe you'd like to try a new adventure, like skiing or rafting. Maybe you'd like to take a pottery class. You and your family can experience something new together and can learn and grow with each other!

Thanks, and have a great week!

THINK BEFORE ACTING

Monday: Recognition and Inspiration

We would first like to congratulate last week's *Students of the Week,* from who met our goal of *trying something new.*

This week, your goal as a student at _____ School is to *think before acting.* Thinking before acting takes practice and self-control. It is easy to act rashly and quickly, and we may later wish that we could go back and change what we have done. That isn't possible, so the best thing to do is to stop, take a breath, think about different options, think about consequences, and make the best choice. Thinking before acting will save you a world of trouble! *Think before acting* today!

Tuesday: Why Should We Think Before We Act?

Thinking before we act prevents us from doing things we'll later regret. When we think before acting, we can consider the effects of our behavior, the way someone else will feel, the consequences of the behavior, and other choices we can make. Thinking before acting takes discipline. It is very easy to respond quickly when we are angry or upset, but our first reaction is not usually a very good one. By stepping back and thinking for a few minutes, we can usually come up with better options. Make sure you *think before acting* today!

Wednesday: Role Model

Our role model for this week is Anfernee "Penny" Hardaway, a professional basketball player. He grew up in Memphis, Tennessee and attended college there. Anfernee often needed to think before he acted, and he was able to avoid violence, stay out of trouble, and stay away from alcohol and drugs. Because Anfernee was able to think about his actions and did not fall into things that could have hurt his career in basketball, he has gone on to achieve success in the NBA. *Think before acting* today!

Thursday: At Home

At home you can practice thinking before acting with your brothers and sisters. We often let our guard down with our families, and sometimes that means that we do not pay enough attention to what we say and do. This can lead to a lot of hurt feelings and fights between brothers and sisters. Think about the number of times your brother or sister has said something that made you very angry. Did you react in a way that helped the situation or made it worse? Stop and think about your options tonight before you react. Don't make a problem worse for you or for anyone else.

180 Daily Guidance Lessons To Jump-Start Your Day! © 2007 Mar∗co Products, Inc. 1.800.448.2197

Friday: What Would You Do?

Harrison: I cannot believe I have to go over there to say something to him. I'm sick of his meanness. Who does he think he is?

Joel: What are you planning on saying? Anything you say is going to cause a problem. Why don't you calm down first? I'll help you pick everything up.

Harrison: I *know* he did it on purpose. I'm going to go over there and make him pick up every one of these books. Just watch and see.

Joel: Harrison, take a deep breath and think about this. First of all, he probably didn't mean to do it. Secondly, if you go over there, you are going to end up in a fight and get into big trouble.

What would you do?

Classroom Activity

Stop Signs: With red construction paper, help your students create their own personal stop signs. Describe different scenarios to the class and have the students hold up their signs when the person in the scenario should "stop" and think. Let the students use their stop signs as reminders of when they need to stop and think about their actions.

180 Daily Guidance Lessons To Jump-Start Your Day! © 2007 Mar∗co Products, Inc. 1.800.448.2197

LETTER TO PARENTS/GUARDIANS
WEEK 26: THINK BEFORE ACTING

Dear Parents/Guardians:

As part of JUMP-START! this week, we are focusing on *thinking before acting*. Thinking before we act prevents bullying because it helps us to not act rashly or violently or in anger—the kind of actions we often regret later. Thinking before acting is something that children and adults need to practice. Talk with your child about the benefits of thinking before he/she acts: not getting into as much trouble, having fewer problems with friends, making better decisions, etc. Explain to your child that it is not easy to think before acting, and that it takes discipline and practice. Praise your child when you see him/her thinking before acting.

Fun Family Tip:

◎ With your child, play a game, such as checkers, that requires thinking and concentration. Encourage your child to "stop" and "think" before taking his/her turn. When playing games, children are often so excited to take their turns that they don't stop and think about what they are doing. This is a great, fun way to practice self-discipline and thinking before acting!

Thanks, and have a great week!

DO SOMETHING YOU LOVE

Monday: Recognition and Inspiration

We would first like to congratulate last week's *Students of the Week*, who met our goal of *thinking before acting.*

This week, your goal as a student at _____ School is to *do something you love*. Doing something you love sounds like a simple thing to do—and it is! But we don't often think about doing something because it's something *we* love or that *we* want to do. Instead, we often do what seems to be the popular thing to do or the thing our friends are telling us to do. What do you love? Is it reading? Is it drawing? Is it playing a game? Think about something you love, and do it today.

Tuesday: Why Should We Do Something We Love?

Doing something we love helps prevent us from giving in to peer pressure, which often results in bullying. By doing things we love, we are being independent people who are able to make our own decisions. Think about the things *you* love to do, not the things your group of friends wants to do. If you love cooking, make sure you cook. If you love gardening, get outside and plant something. If you love comics, spend some time reading your comics. Remember that you are a unique person with different interests than other people. *Do what you love* today!

Wednesday: Role Model

Our role model for this week is Arthur Ashe, a famous tennis player who won Wimbledon, the US Open, the French Open, and the Canadian Open. Arthur Ashe did something he loved not only to achieve success in sports, but to further the Civil Rights Movement. Later in his life, he brought attention to AIDS sufferers around the world and founded the Arthur Ashe Institute for Urban Health. Arthur Ashe pursued something he loved—tennis. And through tennis, he was able to help change our world. Make sure you *do something you love* today!

Thursday: At Home

At home tonight, do something you love to do but have not done for a while. Maybe you think you have outgrown something you love to do or that your friends would laugh at you if they knew about it. Take advantage of being at your house and give yourself some happiness by doing something you have not done lately. Maybe you still like to watch a cartoon that you think you are too old for. Watch it, and have a great time. Maybe you are missing your dolls, but think you are too old to enjoy them. Dress them up and remember how much fun you have had playing with them. *Do something you love*—something that you have been missing—tonight.

Friday: What Would You Do?

Yvonne: Why do you have all those stickers in your backpack?

Carly: I collect stickers. I have more than 1,000 stickers. You should see them! They're really cool.

Yvonne: Why would I want to look at stickers? That doesn't seem like much fun. I can't believe you waste your time collecting stickers. I'd much rather be painting my fingernails with this great new polish I got yesterday.

Carly: I've been collecting stickers for a while. I really like them.

Yvonne: You need to grow up! Stickers are not very exciting.

What would you do?

Classroom Activity

Bar Graphs: Have your students make bar graphs of the five things they most love to do and shade in the amount of time they spend on each activity. Have each student present his/her graph to the class. Display the graphs in the classroom.

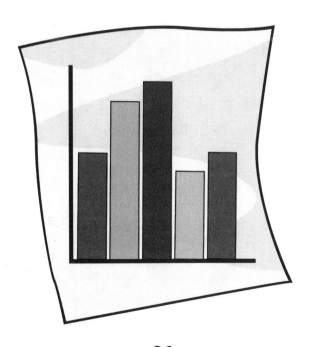

91

JUMP-START!

**LETTER TO PARENTS/GUARDIANS
WEEK 27: DO SOMETHING YOU LOVE**

Dear Parents/Guardians:

As part of JUMP-START! this week, we are focusing on *doing things we love.* Doing things we love promotes independence, which prevents people from succumbing to peer pressuring. We often forget about the things we love to do and, instead, do the things our friends are doing. It is important that children and adults spend time doing things they enjoy doing. Talk with your child about things he/she loves to do. Children are often embarrassed about things they enjoy doing because they think the activities are too babyish or that their friends will laugh at them. Encourage your child to continue to enjoy these activities as long as they make him/her happy.

Fun Family Tip:

◎ Talk with your child about something you loved to do when you were a child and do it together. For example, maybe you loved fishing as a child. Share this experience with your child. Then allow your child to share with you an activity that he/she loves to do. You and your child can respect and enjoy each other's activities.

Thanks, and have a great week!

HAVE AN OPEN MIND

Monday: Recognition and Inspiration

We would first like to congratulate last week's *Students of the Week,* who met our goal of *doing something they love.*

This week, your goal as a student at _____ School is to *have an open mind.* Having an open mind means not making judgments about people before getting to know them. Having an open mind means being open to new experiences. People who are open-minded are tolerant of others' opinions and interests. Be open-minded in your decisions today. It will help you learn more about the people and the world around you!

Tuesday: Why Should We Have an Open Mind?

Having an open mind helps people treat each other fairly and with respect. People who are open-minded are tolerant of others and do not judge them. Having an open mind means not being prejudiced and not discriminating against others. Before you make a decision about someone, make sure that you are not basing this decision on the way he/she looks or dresses. Instead of judging each person you encounter, give him/her a chance. You may be surprised to find people right around you who are funny, smart, and can be good friends. You just have to give them a chance. *Have an open mind* today!

Wednesday: Role Model

Our role model for this week is Jackie Robinson, the first African-American to play in major league baseball. This angered many people, but Jackie Robinson's professionalism, dedication to baseball, and record-breaking athletic accomplishments helped open the minds of people all over America. After retiring from baseball, Jackie Robinson continued to support the Civil Rights Movement and the fight against racism. *Have an open mind* today!

Thursday: At Home

At home you can be open-minded toward your sisters and brothers. You and your brothers and sisters are not exactly alike. You probably do not look the same, and you probably have many different interests. Be open-minded and tolerant of their interests and opinions. Many disagreements with your siblings may disappear if you treat each other with respect and tolerance. You don't have to agree with someone's opinion—you just have to respect it. Let your open-mindedness improve your relationship with your brothers and sisters today.

180 Daily Guidance Lessons To Jump-Start Your Day! © 2007 Mar∗co Products, Inc. 1.800.448.2197

Friday: What Would You Do?

Mena: What is that thing Jade is wearing? She looks like a bag lady! I don't know where she gets those weird clothes.

Tess: Jade is actually pretty interesting. Yesterday, I was talking with her about music. She knows a lot about music. She offered to let me borrow some of her CDs.

Mena: Why were you talking with Jade? I wouldn't want to be seen talking with her. People might think you're weird, too.

What would you do?

Classroom Activity

Vocabulary Builder: Define the words: *discrimination, prejudice, unfairness, intolerance, unbiased, impartial, biased, judgment, respect,* and *objective.* Then have the students use each word in a sentence. Discuss how each word is related to *open-mindedness.*

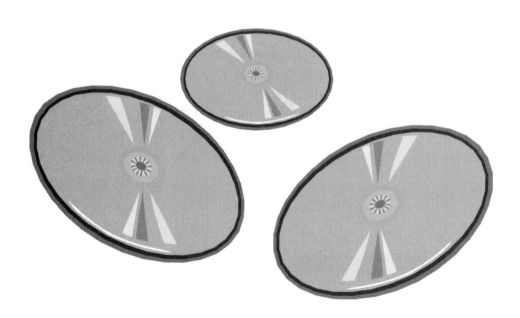

LETTER TO PARENTS/GUARDIANS
WEEK 28: HAVE AN OPEN MIND

Dear Parents/Guardians:

As part of JUMP-START! this week, we are focusing on *having an open mind.* Having an open mind helps us treat each other fairly and with respect. Open-mindedness prevents judgment and discrimination. Many of us don't realize how quickly we form judgments about others. We have to be very careful to really get to know others before making decisions about them. Encourage your child to be open-minded with others.

Fun Family Tip:

◎ For a quick lesson in open-mindedness, try this at dinner one night: Tell your family that dinner will be a food that you like, but one that your children do not like. Tell your family that from now on, you will be having this food for dinner because it is your favorite. Explain that if you like it, everyone else has to like it, too. Of course, you will hear many complaints of how unfair this is! After a few minutes, tell everyone that this is a joke, and a little lesson in open-mindedness. Even though you love this food, you are open-minded and understand that not everyone else loves it or would want to eat it every day!

Thanks, and have a great week!

MAKE SOMEONE'S DAY

Monday: Recognition and Inspiration

We would first like to congratulate last week's *Students of the Week,* who met our goal of *having an open mind.*

This week, your goal as a student at _____ School is to *make someone's day.* Making someone's day means trying to do something that will help ensure that someone has a fabulous day. Making someone's day requires being unselfish and reaching out to someone else. Maybe you'd like to write a nice note thanking your teacher for being so helpful. Maybe you'd like to let one of your friends borrow something of yours that he/she has been wanting to use for a while. *Make someone's day* today!

Tuesday: Why Should We Make Someone's Day?

Making someone's day helps us to act unselfishly and think about the needs and the happiness of others. People who are concerned about helping someone else are unlikely to engage in bullying behaviors. Helping someone else have a great day can be a wonderful experience for us as well as for the person we help. Making someone's day need not take much time or cost any money. Making someone's day requires thoughtfulness. Think about something that would make one of your friends happy today and take the time to do it. You will be amazed at how happy it will make you, too!

Wednesday: Role Model

Our role model for this week is Erin Puck. As a 13-year old battling brain cancer, Erin began collecting stuffed animals for other hospitalized children. Concerned about other children and how they were feeling, Erin decided to make their days a little better. By giving them stuffed animals, Erin was able to give them some comfort and some fun. Toys Calm, which Erin founded, has distributed more than 75,000 books, toys, games, and laptop computers to hospitals in Erin's home state of New Jersey and in other states. Be like Erin and *make someone's day* today!

Thursday: At Home

At home you can help make your parents' day by doing something to help them out tonight. Offer to clean the kitchen or the living room while your parents relax after dinner. Helping your parents takes very little time and they'll be thrilled. Your unselfish act will definitely make their day, and their happiness will satisfy you, too! Help your parents have a great night tonight.

Friday: What Would You Do?

Yolanda: Hurry up and finish your work so we can go outside for recess.

Desiree: I don't think I'm going out to recess today. I offered to help the music teacher set the stage up for the choral concert.

Yolanda: Why would you do that? She can set it up by herself or she can get somebody else to help her. Come on! Let's go outside!

Desiree: I know she's been so busy trying to get everything ready, and she's been working so hard for us to have a great concert for our families. I wanted to do something to help her have a good day today.

Yolanda: Well, I think you shouldn't worry about it. She's the teacher, and it's her job to set everything up.

What would you do?

Classroom Activity

Appreciation Day: Each day this week, pick a different school employee and have your students make that person's day. For your school custodian, for example, take some extra time to make sure your class is neat and orderly. Your students can make a card thanking the custodian for keeping the school clean. Your students could make a card for the cafeteria workers and take extra time to clean their table and the area around it. Brainstorm with your class about different ways to show thankfulness and different ways to make someone's day at your school!

180 Daily Guidance Lessons To Jump-Start Your Day! © 2007 Mar★co Products, Inc. 1.800.448.2197

JUMP-START!

Dear Parents/Guardians:

As part of JUMP-START! this week, we are focusing on *making someone's day.* Making someone's day helps us reach out to others. Making someone's day requires thinking about others' feelings and needs. It need not cost money or take much time. It *does* require thoughtfulness. It is wonderful to see how happy you can make someone by giving a little bit of your time and attention. Help your child think of ways he/she can help make someone happy. Encourage your child to help someone have a great day.

Fun Family Tip:

◎ As a family, surprise a neighbor, friend, or relative by completing a chore such as raking leaves, mowing the grass, or washing the car for him/her. Your family will benefit from the joy of helping someone else! Talk with your family about the importance of helping others.

Thanks, and have a great week!

THINK POSITIVE THOUGHTS

Monday: Recognition and Inspiration

We would first like to congratulate last week's *Students of the Week,* who met our goal of *making someone's day.*

This week, your goal as a student at _____ School is to *think positive thoughts.* It is easy to get dragged down by negative thoughts and complaints. We have to make the decision to not complain and to stop thinking negative thoughts as soon as we begin thinking them. Instead, concentrate on positive thoughts such as how you will achieve a goal and how you will have a great day at school. Tell yourself that you love math and that you are great in reading. Tell yourself that you are great at basketball and in art. Fill yourself with positive thoughts today.

Tuesday: Why Should We Think Positive Thoughts?

Thinking positive thoughts helps stop us from thinking negative things about ourselves and others. Thinking negative things about ourselves lowers our self-esteem and increases our anger. Negative thoughts about others can also increase anger, as well as jealousy, bitterness, and hatred. In order to think positive thoughts, you must tell yourself that you are smart, that you are good in sports, that you are a great friend, that you are a good son or daughter, or that you can achieve anything today!

Wednesday: Role Model

Our role model for this week is Christopher Reeve, an actor whose most famous role was that of *Superman.* In 1995, Christopher Reeve was thrown from a horse and became paralyzed from the neck down. He faced this trauma with courage and hope and focused on rehabilitation and learning how to do everything with the help of a wheelchair and other aids. Christopher Reeve did not give up on himself or on others. He brought attention to spinal cord research and founded the Christopher Reeve Foundation, which helps improve the quality of life of disabled individuals. Don't give up. Make sure you *think positive thoughts* today!

Thursday: At Home

At home you can practice thinking positive thoughts about one of your hobbies or a sport you like to play. Trying to learn something new is always frustrating, and everyone struggles. You must tell yourself that you're doing a great job and that you're talented. Don't give up or let negative thoughts creep in. The better you feel about yourself, the better job you will do. *Think positive thoughts* about your favorite activity today.

180 Daily Guidance Lessons To Jump-Start Your Day! © 2007 Mar*co Products, Inc. 1.800.448.2197

Friday: What Would You Do?

Portia: I am so sick of history! I just *cannot* learn this stuff. I can't wait until summer. I'm not sure I'm even going to pass.

Mena: Portia, you're going to be fine. You are so smart! You just need to review the material. You can definitely do it.

Portia: Don't say that! You know you're sick of school, too. Everyone hates it.

Mena: I'm going to miss everyone at school when summer gets here. And I really like our teachers.

Portia: You are so weird. I don't know how you can say that.

What would you do?

Classroom Activity

Positive-Thought Chart: Make a positive-thought chart for your classroom. Have students brainstorm about positive thoughts such as, "I am smart," "I am talented," "I am great in writing," "I am a fast runner," etc. Try to fill the chart with positive thoughts. Display the chart in your classroom, pointing out a few thoughts each day.

180 Daily Guidance Lessons To Jump-Start Your Day! © 2007 Mar✳co Products, Inc. 1.800.448.2197

JUMP-START!

LETTER TO PARENTS/GUARDIANS
WEEK 30: THINK POSITIVE THOUGHTS

Dear Parents/Guardians:

As part of JUMP-START! this week, we are focusing on *thinking positive thoughts.* Thinking positive thoughts helps us feel good about ourselves and about others. When we think negative thoughts about ourselves and others, we feel angry, jealous, discontented, and aggressive. Encourage your child to think positive thoughts about him/herself and about others. Tell your child how smart and talented he/she is. When your child becomes discouraged about problems with friends, sports, or school, continue to praise him/her and encourage your child not to give up.

Fun Family Tip:

◎ Have your children draw self-portraits. Underneath each portrait, help the artist write five positive statements about him/herself. Hang the portraits in your children's rooms to remind them of their positive qualities.

Thanks, and have a great week!

DO YOUR BEST

Monday: Recognition and Inspiration

We would first like to congratulate last week's *Students of the Week,* who met our goal of *thinking positive thoughts.*

This week, your goal as a student at _____ School is to *do your best.* Doing our best means giving everything 100%, even when we don't feel like it. It means that we try to succeed in everything we do, even the activities we don't enjoy. Amaze your teacher today by doing your best in all your subjects. Do your best by paying attention and working hard. Do your best in sports and with your friends. Have a great day and *do your best!*

Tuesday: Why Should We Do Our Best?

Doing our best helps us become more responsible for our own actions. By doing our best, we can help prevent arguments with friends. You can do your best and make sure that you do not pick on others. You can do your best by telling an adult if you know about someone being bullied. Doing your best requires that you do the right thing, no matter what. Even if others are not doing so, and even if you don't want to do it. Doing your best is what responsible people do. Make sure you *do your best* today.

Wednesday: Role Model

Our role model for this week is Ellen Ochoa, the first female Hispanic astronaut. In order to be an astronaut, you have to do your best and excel in many areas. Ellen Ochoa worked hard to become an astronaut, and went on to become an inventor and a scientist for NASA. Ellen Ochoa is a great example of someone who has worked hard and done her best. *Do your best* today!

Thursday: At Home

At home you can do your best by doing a great job in everything you do. When you are playing with your brothers and sisters, do you best to get along with them. This will prevent fights and help everyone in your house be happy. When you are doing your chores, do your best to do them well. Don't do a sloppy job. Do your chores right the first time. Take your time with your homework and do your best. Your responsible actions will please your parents. Show off your skills of *doing your best* tonight!

Friday: What Would You Do?

Michaela: I am hurrying to finish my homework so I can watch my favorite show on TV.

Nadia: How are you doing with your math? I had a hard time doing my homework. My mom is going to help me work on it some more after dinner.

Michaela: I don't really care. I just want to finish so I can watch TV. I'll worry about math tomorrow. The teacher never really checks it anyway.

Nadia: I want my mom to help me so I can do a good job. It's a waste of time for me to just put down answers. If I do, I'll have to learn it later and by then I'll get further behind. I don't want that to happen.

What would you do?

Classroom Activity

Class Discussion: Ask the students:

- What are some activities that you don't like to do? Is it hard to do your best in these activities? Explain why or why not.
- Talk about some activities in which you do your best. Why do you think you do your best in these activities?
- How do you think people can tell if you have done your best in an activity?
- Do you think it matters if you do your best in an activity? Why or why not?
- Do you think people really pay attention when they hear someone say, "Do your best"?
- What do you think helps inspire people to do their best?

103

JUMP-START!

LETTER TO PARENTS/GUARDIANS
WEEK 31: DO YOUR BEST

Dear Parents/Guardians:

As part of JUMP-START! this week, we are focusing on doing our best. Doing our best helps us act responsibly. People who do their best try to get along with others, stand up for others, and work hard at everything they do. People who do their best do the right thing, whether they feel like it or not, despite what others may say. Encourage your child to do his/her best in everything he/she does. It is easy for us to do our best in things we love. The real test is if we do our best in activities that we do not enjoy.

Fun Family Tip:

◎ Discuss the quote from Abraham Lincoln, the 16th American president, "Whatever you are, be a good one." These words are simple—yet packed with meaning. Talk with your family about what this quote means to them at this point in their lives.

Thanks, and have a great week!

DON'T GIVE UP

Monday: Recognition and Inspiration

We would first like to congratulate last week's *Students of the Week,* who met our goal of *doing your best*.

This week, your goal as a student at _____ School is to *not give up*. Not giving up requires that we persevere, which means that we continue trying even when it seems like there is no hope that we'll succeed. Many people become easily discouraged and give up when they begin to have a hard time. Maybe you are struggling in English or some other subject and just don't get it. Don't give up. Keep going. Step back, take a deep breath, and continue to do your best. Maybe you are having a hard time making friends. Don't quit trying. Talk to your counselor, your teacher, your mom or dad, or another adult. Think about students who are nice and reach out to them. Make sure you *don't give up* today!

Tuesday: Why Should We Not Give Up?

Not giving up keeps us from getting too frustrated to do anything about a difficult situation. If you are being picked on or bullied, do not give up—get adult help. If you know of someone who is being picked on, do not feel like there is nothing you can do. You can stand up for that person and be his/her friend or you can get adult help. If someone is lonely and seems to have no friends, do not give up or think it's not your problem. You can help by talking with this person and reaching out to him/her. One of the worst things you can do is sit back and do nothing. Make sure you that you *don't give up* today!

Wednesday: Role Model

Our role model for this week is Thomas Edison, one of the greatest inventors in our history. One of his most famous inventions was the light bulb. Thomas Edison tested many different versions of the light bulb before finally creating one that worked. Imagine what our world would be like if he had given up and stopped after the first few attempts. Be like Thomas Edison and *don't give up* today!

Thursday: At Home

At home you can make sure that you don't give up on something you are learning to do. Starting to learn to do something can be extremely frustrating. When someone first learns to play a musical instrument, for example, he/she has to practice notes, chords, and keys. Most people don't pick up a guitar for the first time and immediately begin playing a song. If you give up in the beginning stages, you will never reach the point of playing the whole song. So

105

tonight, pick up something you thought you could never learn to do and begin again. Whether it's music, a game, a sport, or a craft—just *don't give up.*

Friday: What Would You Do?

Trey: Do you want to come over and practice soccer?

Austin: No, I think I'm going to stay here and practice running. I was getting ready to do some sprints. Do you want to run with me?

Trey: I don't want to run with you. You are way too slow. Why are you running? That is really funny. You're the slowest guy in our class.

Austin: I'm practicing and trying to get faster.

Trey: I think you should just give that up and come over and practice kicking.

What would you do?

Classroom Activity

Goal Chart: Have each student in your class draw a picture of something he/she is trying to do (learn soccer, improve in math, make more friends, etc). Have each student create a monthly chart at the bottom of the picture. Each week, the students may fill in the charts with different ways that they worked toward this goal. At the end of the month, students may share their pictures and charts with the class.

180 Daily Guidance Lessons To Jump-Start Your Day! © 2007 Mar∗co Products, Inc. 1.800.448.2197

JUMP-START!

LETTER TO PARENTS/GUARDIANS
WEEK 32: DON'T GIVE UP

Dear Parents/Guardians:

As part of JUMP-START! this week, we are focusing on *not giving up*. Not giving up helps us persevere and keep trying, no matter what. If someone is bullying, for example, students should not assume there is nothing they can do about it. They should seek adult help. If someone is being picked on, students should not give up. They should either talk with an adult or assert themselves.

Encourage your child to not give up when he/she is trying something new. Everyone gets frustrated when learning something. With patience and determination, we can learn a new skill, but it may not happen quickly.

Fun Family Tip:

◎ Teach your child a new game, such as a card game, checkers, or chess. When teaching your child, encourage him/her to not give up or become discouraged. Explain that it is always hard to learn something new. Have fun with your game and praise your child for not giving up!

Thanks, and have a great week!

START OVER

Monday: Recognition and Inspiration

We would first like to congratulate last week's *Students of the Week,* who met our goal of *not giving up.*

This week, your goal as a student at _____ School is to *start over.* When we're having a difficult time with something, we don't always know how to stop and change directions. It is never to late to start over—whether with your studies or your grades or your relationships with your teachers, your parents, or your friends.

Tuesday: Why Should We Start Over?

Starting over helps us change negative behaviors. We often believe we are stuck with a certain behavior or label. Maybe you believe everyone thinks you're a troublemaker. Instead of continuing with behaviors that cause trouble, you can stop these behaviors and start over with new, positive behaviors. If you have been having fights with some of your friends, approach them with a new attitude and let go of whatever has been bothering you lately. Remember that it's never too late to *start over!*

Wednesday: Role Model

Our role model for starting over is Bethany Hamilton. In 2003, 13-year old Bethany was surfing in Hawaii when she was attacked by a shark. Bethany survived, but her arm could not be saved. Instead of giving up on surfing, Bethany started over and learned a new way to surf using only one arm. Less than a month after her accident, Bethany began surfing again. She has won several competitions and earned a spot on the U.S. National Surfing Team. Be like Bethany and don't be afraid to *start over* today!

Thursday: At Home

At home you can start over with something that has been troubling you with your parents or your brothers or sisters. If your brother or sister has been making you angry, don't keep thinking about it and getting mad, let go of it and start over again today. You may be surprised at how much better you feel if you can forgive and forget. If you have been getting into trouble with your parents, don't feel like all is lost or that it is too late to change. Remember that it is never too late to change and start anew. Try it tonight!

180 Daily Guidance Lessons To Jump-Start Your Day! © 2007 Mar∗co Products, Inc. 1.800.448.2197

Friday: What Would You Do?

India: I'm so tired of dealing with Jill! She and I have been friends for a long time, but lately we've been fighting every day.

Sydney: Why are you guys fighting?

India: I don't even *know* why we're fighting. She is just being mean, and I can't take it any more.

Sydney: Why don't you try starting over with her? Maybe you guys just need to forget about everything that's been happening and have a fresh start.

What would you do?

Classroom Activity

Class Discussion: Have the students talk about times when they had a problem with some-one, then apologized and worked things out. Ask:

- Why do you think it is difficult for people to let go of problems and start over?
- What things do you think help make it easier for friends to work out problems?
- Talk about some times when you wish you had stopped doing something and started over. Why do you think you did not start over? What do you think would have happened if you had stopped and started over?

180 Daily Guidance Lessons To Jump-Start Your Day! © 2007 Mar✶co Products, Inc. 1.800.448.2197

JUMP-START!

LETTER TO PARENTS/GUARDIANS
WEEK 33: START OVER

Dear Parents/Guardians:

As part of JUMP-START! this week, we are focusing on *starting over*. We often get accustomed to acting a certain way and may start to believe we are "bad" or "mean" or "not smart." For example, starting over prevents bullying because it helps people change behaviors. Sometimes we feel we cannot do something, like play baseball or read. We feel like failures and are afraid to start over. Make sure your child knows that it is never too late to make a fresh start.

Fun Family Tip:

◎ Play a quick game of "Mother, May I?" or "Red Light/Green Light" with your children. Each time your children forget to say "Mother, May I?" or are caught going forward during the "Red Light," they must go back to the beginning and start over. Children can see that starting over is an easy thing to do and is still a fun part of the game. Children can also see that they can easily catch up to others in the game and need not be afraid of starting over.

Thanks, and have a great week!

FORGIVE OTHERS

Monday: Recognition and Inspiration

We would first like to congratulate last week's *Students of the Week,* who met our goal of *starting over.*

This week, your goal as a student at _____ School is to *forgive others.* Forgiving others is easy to say, but hard to do. When we have problems with other people, we need to forgive them, even if they have done something wrong. If we hold onto that anger, it only ends up hurting us. If someone apologizes to us, we need to accept the apology and make a fresh start. If we don't forgive and we keep thinking about or bringing up old problems, we will never be able to mend a friendship. Try to let go of your anger and really *forgive others* today.

Tuesday: Why Should We Forgive Others?

Forgiving others stops us from holding onto anger. People who harbor anger can become bitter and may stop caring how others feel. By forgiving others and letting go of negative feelings, we can improve friendships and reduce conflict. It is very difficult to let go of anger and really forgive. We have to make a decision to forgive, even if we don't feel like it. If you choose to hold onto the anger, you will only hurt yourself and others. Make sure you *forgive others* today.

Wednesday: Role Model

Our role models for this week are the members of the United Nations. The UN, as it is known, was formed at the end of World War II in hopes of promoting peace and preventing future conflicts between countries. Today, there are 192 member states of the UN. Many of these countries have been at war with one another in the past. In order to work together to achieve peace, people must forgive and move on. Make sure you *forgive others* as well!

Thursday: At Home

At home you can show your forgiveness of others by being nice to your brother or sister, even if he/she just did something that made you really angry. Forgive him/her and move on. Don't let the problem get you down and keep you angry. By forgiving your brother or sister, you will help reduce fights, which will promote peace in your house. Your parents will be happier, your brothers and sisters will be happier, and you will be happier. Try it tonight!

180 Daily Guidance Lessons To Jump-Start Your Day! © 2007 Mar*co Products, Inc. 1.800.448.2197

Friday: What Would You Do?

Lena: Hey, Trisha, what are you doing?

Trisha: I'm getting ready to go talk with Sari.

Lena: I thought you and Sari were fighting.

Trisha: Well, we were having some problems, but we worked it all out.

Lena: What do you mean, you worked it all out? Aren't you still mad at Sari? I would still be mad at her if I were you. She said some pretty rough stuff to you.

Trisha: I'm not going to worry about that any more. That's all in the past. I forgave her.

What would you do?

Classroom Activity

Paper Bag Puppet Show: Have your students make people puppets out of paper bags. Divide your class into small groups. Instruct each group to create a puppet show which portrays working out a problem and forgiving each other. Have the students perform the puppet shows for the class.

180 Daily Guidance Lessons To Jump-Start Your Day! © 2007 Mar✶co Products, Inc. 1.800.448.2197

JUMP-START!

LETTER TO PARENTS/GUARDIANS
WEEK 34: FORGIVE OTHERS

Dear Parents/Guardians:

As part of JUMP-START! this week, we are focusing on *forgiving others.* Forgiving others helps us let go of anger and let go of conflicts with others. By holding onto anger, we end up fighting, we end up in trouble, we end up hurting ourselves and others, and we remain angry. Forgiving others is difficult to do, but we must do it, even when we still feel angry. Encourage your child to be mature and forgive others. Explain that once someone has apologized, everyone should make a fresh start. Praise your child when you see him/her forgiving others.

Fun Family Tip:

◎ The next time your child does something wrong and apologizes and you say, "It's OK," spend some time explaining that those words mean that the incident is over, that you forgive your child, and that you will not stay angry. Even though some behaviors have natural consequences or punishments, explain that you still forgive and love your child— and that nothing can change that. Encourage your child to forgive others in the same manner.

Thanks, and have a great week!

ACHIEVE A GOAL

Monday: Recognition and Inspiration

We would first like to congratulate last week's *Students of the Week,* who met our goal of *forgiving others.*

This week, your goal as a student at _____ School is *to achieve a goal.* Everyone should set goals and strive to achieve them whether they involve sports, crafts, household chores, friends, or anyone or anything else. You may set goals to improve your grades, to get into less trouble, to be a better friend, to learn to sew, or to learn to skate. Just make sure to set a goal you'd like to achieve. Start working to *achieve that goal!*

Tuesday: Why Should We Achieve A Goal?

Achieving a goal helps us feel good about ourselves, which improves our self-esteem. Working to achieve a goal motivates us, which keeps us busy and excited. People who are busy, motivated, excited, and feeling good about themselves are less likely to bully others. Think of a goal that you would like to achieve. It doesn't have to be a huge goal. It can be something very small, like remembering to bring your pencils to school. Think of something you would like to accomplish. Set this as your goal, then break it down into small steps. Begin working on the first small step today, and you are on your way to *achieving your goal!*

Wednesday: Role Model

Our role model for this week is Lance Armstrong, the famous cyclist who has won the Tour de France an amazing seven times. One of the most unbelievable things about Lance Armstrong is that his wins of the Tour de France took place after battling cancer. Lance went on to achieve great goals, despite difficulties, and to establish the Lance Armstrong Foundation to inspire and empower people affected by cancer. Be like Lance and *achieve your goals!*

Thursday: At Home

At home you can achieve goals by picking something you and your family can work on together. For a family goal, you might want to pick something fun to do, like learning to do a craft or play a game. Or you might want to have a goal like eating more fruits and vegetables. Come up with a goal that you and your family can work on and achieve together. It is often easier and more fun to work on a goal with others than to work on it alone. Work with your family tonight!

Friday: What Would You Do?

Shannon: What are you doing outside, Gary?

Gary: I'm out here with my soccer ball.

Shannon: It's kind of dark out here. Don't you want to come inside and watch a movie?

Gary: Not right now. I'm trying to become a better soccer player.

Shannon: Well, I think you should come in and watch TV with me. You can practice later.

What would you do?

Classroom Activity

Class Discussion: Ask the students:

- What are some characteristics and traits of people who are successful at achieving goals?
- Why do you think these characteristics and traits help people achieve their goals?
- What characteristic do you think will help you achieve goals? How will it help you?
- What characteristics do you need to improve so you can do a better job of achieving your goals?

115

JUMP-START!

LETTER TO PARENTS/GUARDIANS
WEEK 35: ACHIEVE A GOAL

Dear Parents/Guardians:

As part of JUMP-START! this week, we are focusing on *achieving a goal.* Achieving a goal motivates us and makes us successful, which builds self-esteem and confidence. The better we feel about ourselves, the less likely we are to harass others and the less likely we are to not stand up for ourselves. Achieving goals requires determination and the belief that we can succeed. Encourage your child to set a goal that can be easily met and help him/her reach it. Then encourage him/her to set more difficult goals and help your child make a plan to achieve them.

Fun Family Tip:

◎ Make a goal book with your child. Children and even adults often become overwhelmed when they look at the big picture and think about all the steps required to reach a goal. Help your child set a goal, then break the goal into five steps. Fold paper and staple it together to make a book with seven pages. On the first page, write the goal. On each of the next five pages, write one of the steps your child will take to achieve that goal. On the last page, write "Goal achieved!" Fold the book so that only the goal shows. Hang the book in a place where your child can see it. Let him/her work on taking only the first step. When that step is achieved, make a big check mark on the top of that page and reward your child. Continue doing this until each step has been completed and your child has achieved his/her goal!

Thanks, and have a great week!

TALK

Monday: Recognition and Inspiration

We would first like to congratulate last week's *Students of the Week,* who met our goal of *achieving a goal.*

This week, your goal as a student at _____ School is to *talk*. That seems like a weird goal, but talking is actually a wonderful, powerful goal for everyone to have. Without talking, we can't work out problems. Without talking, we can't reach out to someone who is hurting. Without talking, we can't laugh and joke with our friends. Without talking, we can't tell our parents we love them. Use your words in a positive way today!

Tuesday: Why Should We Talk?

Talking helps us work out problems before they become too big to handle easily. Talking can help us reach out to someone who is lonely and may feel isolated. Talking can help friends share thoughts and feelings. Talking can help parents and kids communicate with each other. It is important that you talk in a positive way and use your words to help others and to improve your relationships. *Talk* it out today!

Wednesday: Role Model

Our role model for this week is Katie Couric, a famous television anchorwoman. Katie Couric is someone many people have enjoyed watching interview and listen to guests on her program. Katie seems to care about the person with whom she is talking. She has good eye contact with her guests, and she smiles at them. In addition to her success with news and reporting, Katie co-founded the National Colorectal Cancer Research Alliance and played a major role in establishing the Jay Monahan Center for Gastrointestinal Health. Use your ability to *talk* to help someone out today!

Thursday: At Home

At home you can spend some time really talking with your brothers and sisters. We don't always think about our brothers and sisters' feelings, thoughts, needs, and daily activities. We sometimes just think they're annoying. Instead of thinking about them as people who get on your nerves, think about them as people, just like you, with real feelings and thoughts. Talk with them about things that are going on with you and with them. It will help you grow closer and it will help prevent some of those annoying times! *Talk* tonight!

180 Daily Guidance Lessons To Jump-Start Your Day! © 2007 Mar*co Products, Inc. 1.800.448.2197

Friday: What Would You Do?

Camryn: I am really angry at Dolly.

Michael: What's the problem?

Camryn: We had an argument a few days ago, and now she just rolls her eyes at me and whispers to other people.

Michael: You guys need to talk.

Camryn: How can we do that?

Michael: You can try to talk with her when she's by herself and not around everyone else. Or you can talk with her with an adult, like the school counselor.

Camryn: I don't know. I think she's just going to keep acting awful toward me. I'm scared I'll make it worse.

Michael: I think it will get worse if you don't try to talk

What would you do?

Classroom Activity

Positive Hello: Stand at the door as your students enter the classroom. Greet each student and give him/her a compliment. Before the student may enter the classroom, he/she must do the same to you. This is a great, quick way for students to practice positive, appropriate ways to talk and a great way to start the day.

LETTER TO PARENTS/GUARDIANS
WEEK 36: TALK

Dear Parents/Guardians:

As part of JUMP-START! this week, we are focusing on *talking*. Talking encourages us to work out problems instead of ignoring them and letting them become worse. Talking also encourages us to reach out to others in need. It is important that your child know appropriate ways to talk with others.

Fun Family Tip:

◎ In order to help your child practice appropriate ways to talk with others, try a few of these role-plays:

- Pretend that you are the friend who says you are not going to be your child's friend any more. Work with your child on appropriate ways to talk with that friend and react to that statement.

- Pretend that your child has a friend who is ignoring him/her and is hanging out with other friends. Help your child think of appropriate times and ways to talk with the friend.

Vary these role-plays as needed to fit circumstances to which your child can best relate.

Thanks, and have a great week!

Shannon Trice Black

Shannon Trice Black is currently working on her doctorate in counseling. She has worked with children in a variety of settings, including schools, mental health facilities, and private practice. She lives in Virginia with her husband and two daughters. She enjoys reading, yoga, movies, and spending time with her friends and family.